# CONVERSATION COMPASS

# Conversation Compass

## A Teacher's Guide to High-Quality Language Learning in Young Children

Stephanie M. Curenton, PhD

Redleaf Press®
www.redleafpress.org
800-423-8309

Published by Redleaf Press
10 Yorkton Court
St. Paul, MN 55117
www.redleafpress.org

First edition 2016
Cover illustrations by ThinkStock/MAKHNACH_M
Interior design by Mayfly Design
Typeset in the Arno Pro and Adoquin Typefaces
Printed in the United States of America

22  21  20  19  18  17  16  15      1  2  3  4  5  6  7  8

Library of Congress Cataloging-in-Publication Data
Curenton, Stephanie M.
  Conversation compass : a teacher's guide to high-quality language learning in young children / Stephanie M. Curenton, PhD. — First edition.
      pages cm
  Includes bibliographical references.
  ISBN 978-1-60554-384-0 (alk. paper)
1. Language arts (Elementary) 2. Conversation—Study and teaching (Elementary) I. Title.
  LB1576.C859 2016
  372.6—dc23
                        2015013739

Printed on acid-free paper

*To the millions of early childhood educators who dedicate their lives
to fostering the healthy growth and development of our nation's youngest children,
and especially to my own Head Start teachers, who saw
the potential in a child like me . . .*

# CONTENTS

# FOREWORD

*Pedagogy must be oriented not to the yesterday, but to the tomorrow of the child's development. Only then can it call to life in the process of education those processes of development which now lie in the zone of proximal development. Therefore, teaching must lead development forward not lag behind. We must teach to the potential.*

L. S. Vygotsky

Teaching to ensure that all children develop their full potential is the mission of all of us in the education field. We chose this profession because we believe in the transformational power of education, especially for children who face challenges due to poverty and other social circumstances. How can we make that happen? What do teachers need to do to fulfill this mission when classrooms are getting more diverse than ever before in the history of the United States and the school readiness gap widens as the population become more diverse? We need beliefs about development and learning that promote success, attitudes that are not deficit-oriented, and knowledge of instructional practices that respect children's cultural ways of knowing (Moll and González 1994). The Conversation Compass has been designed to provide early childhood teachers with a tool that will help you in your journey to become culturally responsive teachers for all children, including those growing up in families from diverse cultures and languages. Teachers using the Conversation Compass strategies will be able to promote conversations that are meaningful by building on children's experiences and acknowledging their diverse speech and communication styles.

The crucial role of language in early development, and its association with school readiness, has been well documented (National Research Council 2000). Using more and richer language in the early childhood classroom encourages children's developmental progress and learning. The Conversation Compass discusses theoretical approaches and concepts and provides practical recommendations and activities. It provides the rationale and the strategies for increasing the frequency and quality of instructional conversations in the classroom. This program is built on the notion that languages are learned based on need, purpose, and function, and that conversations are the mechanism for language learning.

An important feature of the Conversation Compass approach is the inclusion of children who speak African American English in the discussion of strategies to support linguistically diverse children. African American English is one of the most widely spoken English dialects in the United States, and a large percentage of young children enter early childhood programs speaking this dialect (Beneke and Cheatham 2015). Because of classroom emphasis on Standard English, children who speak African American English are at risk to be misdiagnosed and inappropriately referred to special education programs. Thus, it is essential that early childhood teachers acquire the knowledge and skills that will help them be effective teachers of these children. Currently, there are few teacher preparation and professional development materials focusing on preparing teachers to work with children speaking African American English. Usually, the needs of this group of children are not considered when discussing the early education needs of linguistically diverse children. There is no doubt that the Conversation Compass approach will be a valuable resource for early childhood teachers serving children who are African American English speakers as well as other culturally, ethnically, and linguistically diverse children.

—Dina C. Castro, PhD, Velma E. Schmidt Endowed Chair in
Early Childhood Education, University of North Texas

# ACKNOWLEDGMENTS

First and foremost, I thank all of the teachers, center directors, education coordinators, home-visitors, parents, and children who participated in this project over the past several years. Without their participation, this project would not have been possible.

In addition, I thank my research assistants who helped me collect and analyze data: Wilfredo Benitez, Dakota Cintron, Janet Sarpong, Jevonna Morrison, Diana Nora, Yusra Syed, and Shari Gardner. A special note of gratitude goes out to Yusra for envisioning the book cover.

Third, I thank my colleagues who provided advice and suggestions throughout the development process: Debra Sullivan, Ginger Swigart, Laura Justice, Tricia Zucker, Tom Rendon, Brenda Coakley, and Elena Fultz. And I thank Quality Assist for working so diligently to create the online course that accompanies this book.

Lastly, I am grateful to the W. K. Kellogg Foundation for providing the financial support to develop this project, which enabled my vision to come alive.

## Research Notes

The transcripts in this book are derived from real-life classroom conversations across many early childhood programs in several states. The transcripts have been edited for clarity and ease of reading. The names of all the teachers and children who appear in the book have been changed.

# WHY I WROTE THIS BOOK:
# A LETTER TO TEACHERS

Dear Teachers,

As an African American preschooler growing up in the 1970s, I can remember elders in my family whispering, "That child sure is smart!" "She's got *good* sense," and "Stephanie asks so many questions..." My questions and comments became even more frequent, and specific, when I enrolled in the local Head Start program. Being in Head Start awakened me intellectually because my teachers taught me to ask *how* and *why*. These classroom conversations opened my mind, causing me to wonder and seek information about the *what*, *when*, and *where* of objects and events. These conversations even gave me the confidence to guess or predict what might happen or to give my opinion. What I understand now is that my teachers and I were engaging in instructional conversations that were fostering my critical thinking and language skills. Instructional conversations are a road map for children's learning. These conversations, indeed, provided a road map for my educational experiences not only as a child but also as an adult who has taught and studied racial and ethnic minority children who are culturally and/or linguistically diverse.

I believe children only succeed when the adults who are teaching and caring for them have the knowledge, resources, and support they need. This book is a resource that will provide you with that knowledge and support. I have spent the last several years developing this idea, testing it out with teachers, getting feedback from my colleagues, and evaluating it to see if it works. I offer it to you with the hopes that it will inspire you to broaden your teaching practices and enhance your conversations with children.

Sincerely,

Stephanie M. Curenton, PhD

# INTRODUCTION

• • •

*It's wintertime and snow is falling outside the preschool classroom. The children wish they could be outside playing in the snow. A few have their faces longingly pressed against the window, but James and Shemeca sit at the table with Mr. Jose, making snowflakes.*

*"Have either of you ever built a snowman?" Mr. Jose asks.*

*"No," says Shemeca.*

*"I have, I have!" says James.*

*"Tell me about the time you built a snowman, James. Tell me what happened."*

*James eagerly begins his story: "One time I was outside in my cousin's backyard, and it was snowing, snowing, snowing. My cousin said, 'Let's build Frosty the Snowman.' So we patted and patted and made a big ball of snow and then another one and another. And then we found some sticks for his arms, and we used rocks for his eyes and nose and mouth. And then it was finished!"*

*"Wow, that sounds like a cool snowman, James," Mr. Jose praises.*

*"Well, Elsa made a snowman," says Shemeca. "She made Olaf."*

*"If you could make a snowman, what kind of snowman would you make, Shemeca?"*

• • •

All teachers have hopes and expectations for their students, regardless of their students' country of origin, ethnicity, or *home language* (the language or dialect a child speaks at home). For example, you may hope that by the time children leave your classroom, they will be able to ask and answer questions and follow the basic social graces for conversations, like not interrupting while someone is speaking. Or maybe you hope that the conversations you have in your classroom will provide a safe space for children to share their feelings and opinions.

Maybe you hope that by the end of the school year, you will witness growth in your students' vocabulary and ability to share information and express ideas.

In order to bring these hopes and expectations to reality, you can use instructional conversation approaches to create a high-quality language-learning environment in your classroom. Using an instructional conversation approach means talking to children with specific learning objectives in mind. It also means intentionally planning opportunities for children to talk with their peers during small-group learning activities. The Conversation Compass is a unique instructional conversation approach that teachers can use to foster high-quality language learning environments in preschool classrooms.

With support from teachers, young children are capable of having meaningful classroom conversations that foster their social-emotional and academic development. For instance, classroom conversations provide opportunities for children to build their social-emotional reasoning skills by talking about their feelings, ideas, opinions, memories, and personal experiences. Conversations are especially important for children's academic growth. Conversations about literacy topics provide opportunities for children to talk about and understand vocabulary and printed text, as well as to understand the motives, thoughts, and feelings of characters in stories. Classroom conversations also build children's math and sciences skills by providing opportunities for young children to evaluate events, make predictions, and solve problems.

## What Is the Conversation Compass?

The Conversation Compass is a conversation-based instructional approach designed to build children's critical thinking, problem solving, social reasoning, and language skills. The suggestions and ideas for this approach are based on a wide body of research about language and cognitive development, early literacy, children's storytelling, family cultural practices, and classroom dialogue. The approach is intended to foster language and school readiness skills in *all* children, especially ethnic minority children who are culturally and linguistically diverse (CALD), and who may speak a home language that is different from the formal, academic English that is taught in school.

This easy-to-use, fillable workbook is designed to enhance the language-learning environment by providing you with tools to plan classroom conversations. Using the Conversation Compass approach, you can plan classroom conversations that focus on higher-order reasoning and that are peer-based and culturally sensitive. This workbook can be used for independent self-study, during group trainings, or in conjunction with an online course at www.conversationcompass.com. Even after self-study, training, or the course, you can use the workbook as a reference guide and reminder of what you have learned and as a ready-made resource for conversation planning tools and activities.

Reading this book will prepare you to apply this approach in your classroom. The Conversation Compass approach includes a few simple instructional approaches that build on each other to guide your classroom conversations:

**Conversation Feedback Loop:** By practicing feedback loops, you can learn how to keep the flow of a conversation going by asking questions, listening effectively, and repeating or elaborating on what someone has said. See more about these in chapter 1.

**Question Trail:** Understanding the Question Trail helps you choose open-ended questions that will drive children's conceptual knowledge. The questions range in level of difficulty from *who, what, when,* and *where* questions to *how* and *why* questions. See more on this in chapter 1.

**Conversation Compass:** The Compass itself is a visual guide that will remind you of the conceptual reasoning paths that should form the basis of your conversations. It will also serve as a reminder to help you select activities and open-ended questions. More about the compass is covered in chapter 3, which discusses how to use it along with the map to plan classroom conversations.

**Conversation Map:** The Map is a sheet that provides a place for you to write down your learning objectives and plan for the conversation. All the important elements of the Conversation Compass approach are captured on this sheet. There is space for you to jot down the conceptual reasoning path you have chosen, to jot down questions, and to assign children to peer groups for their activities. Chapter 3 talks about how to use the map and compass together to intentionally plan instructional conversations with children.

**Tracking Peer Conversations:** After you have practiced the Conversation Compass approach for a while, it will be important to start tracking children's growth and improvements in conversation skills. This progress-monitoring tool

> ### Bridge from Home to School: It's Exciting to Teach CALD Students!
>
> The first step in bridging the home-school language connection is becoming excited about teaching ethnic minority children from diverse language and cultural backgrounds. Teaching CALD children offers you an opportunity to make an extremely important impact in children's lives. It also provides you with opportunities to grow—both professionally and personally. Do you know that almost everyone across the world speaks at least two languages? Often the first step toward learning a new language comes from social contact with people who speak another language, either through schooling or business transactions. By learning some key words in another language and learning how to interact with families from other cultures, you are expanding your worldview, and you are laying the building blocks for expanding your own language development and future opportunities for work and travel!

is a guide for observing children's peer conversations during play and small-group activities. See more on this in chapter 4.

## Why Is the Conversation Compass Needed?

There is a large body of evidence from early childhood education (ECE) classrooms all over the United States showing that almost all teachers need help with strengthening the language-learning environment in their classrooms. Numerous researchers, program evaluators, and program monitors have used the Classroom Assessment Scoring System developed by Robert Pianta, Karen LaParo, and Bridget Hamre (2008) to observe classroom quality. They have found that teachers need help with language modeling, providing feedback, and using conversations to promote children's concept development. Results from other studies of classroom dialogue show that many teachers' classroom talk relies too much on commands to manage behavior ("Everyone sit down on your bottom and raise your hand if you want to speak"). Or teachers' talk mostly consists of directions during classroom transitions ("Now it is time to clean up. Please put all the blocks away").

Unfortunately, language-learning environments are especially weak in classrooms where the majority of children are living in poverty or in classrooms where children speak a home language or dialect other than the Standard American English taught in school. This is the situation for many students, who are called culturally and linguistically diverse (CALD) learners. CALD learners are young children who are learning a home language(s) different from the language they are learning to use at school. Some teachers are confused about how to foster the communication skills of children who are CALD and so they are seeking conversation approaches and materials to help teach children from these diverse language and ethnic backgrounds. If that's you, the Conversation Compass approach can be a good place to start!

Our country is becoming more ethnically and linguistically diverse. Now is an especially critical time for teachers to learn about fostering strong language-learning environments for ethnic and language minority children. In fact, the upcoming generations of young children will be more ethnically diverse than any prior generation. Teachers have to learn how to bridge the home-to-school connection so that *all* families and children feel welcomed into ECE classrooms.

The good news is that research shows that teachers who get instructional lesson-planning tools and professional development can strengthen their classroom (Pence, Justice, and Wiggins 2008)! Education interventions show that when you enhance the quality of your conversations, children's oral language and literacy skills improve (Cabell et al. 2011; Piasta et al. 2012). You might be reading this book because, like me, you also believe in the power that teachers have to improve the language environment of their classrooms. Together, we can embark on the journey of learning how to create better classroom conversations with your students.

Let the journey begin!

# What Does It Mean to Be a *Good* Conversation Partner?

Have you ever been in a conversation you felt was not going well? Maybe your conversation partner was distracted. Or maybe he didn't understand your point. How did you feel during this conversation?

The art of conversing is a skill that is basic to our human nature. People from all cultural traditions and language backgrounds express their thoughts, feelings, and cultural history through conversations. As humans, we build our social and emotional connections by conversing with other people. Conversations are also critical for building our cognitive skills. In fact, cognitive scientists believe that the human mind is quite sophisticated in unconsciously processing all of the emotional, social, interpersonal, and cognitive information delivered during conversations (Garrod and Pickering 2004). The reason our minds can process all this information so quickly is because humans are hardwired to be conversation partners. In fact, our minds are so attuned to conversations that even infants and toddlers show the beginnings of conversation skills.

## What Are the Hallmarks of a *Good* Conversation?

Have you ever seen the YouTube video of two toddler twins talking? In the video, two toddler brothers are standing in their kitchen enthralled in a lively conversation using their own made-up secret language (also known as *idioglossia*). What makes the video so hilarious is that even though no one can understand the twins' secret language, we can tell that they are having a really *good* conversation. Together, these twins display all the key features of a good conversation:

**Using a shared language:** One of the most important aspects of a conversation is being able to use and understand the same language. Language—its words, phrases, and meaningful sounds—is the foundation for any conversation. In the twins' case, both boys use a secret language only they can understand and speak.

**Being focused on the same topic:** If one person is talking about one thing while another is talking about something else, then the two people are not truly having a conversation at all! If two people cannot agree on a conversation topic, then they usually stop talking to each other. In the twins' case, it is clear the boys are talking about the same topic because their conversation continues for multiple back-and-forth exchanges.

**Taking turns speaking and listening:** One of the important features of conversations is turn-taking, meaning each person alternates between the role of speaker and listener in a conversation. Even the toddler twins do a fine job of turn-taking—one brother speaks while the other listens and then the other brother speaks while the first brother listens. Their conversation flows back and forth because they are taking turns being the speaker and the listener.

**Maintaining eye contact:** Eye contact is an interesting cultural aspect of conversations because what it means can vary across cultures. In the United States, especially within the school environment, looking at the person you are talking to is important because it lets your conversation partner know you are listening. But in some other places and cultures around the world, direct eye contact with one's superiors (parents, teachers, bosses) might be viewed as impolite and disrespectful. Throughout

### Watch the Video of the Talking Twins

There are quite a few entertaining videos of young twins talking to each other. The very popular one I'm referring to in my example is a YouTube video from 2011 called "Talking Twin Babies—Part 2." Check it out for a good laugh!

the video of the twins, the two boys are making eye contact with each other, which shows that they are listening to each other and interested in what is being said.

**Using meaningful gestures:** Gestures can be an important way to support what you are saying. The talking twins display numerous gestures. They shake their heads and use their hands. Each even picks up his feet repeatedly. Maybe they are talking about feet? Or socks? Or stepping on something?

**Using facial expressions to convey emotions:** It is important to use facial expressions in a conversation because it lets people know how you feel about what is being said. The talking twins smile at each other throughout their video and they even giggle a few times. So we can conclude that they are both enjoying the conversation.

The conversation skills that the twins use are important for everyone to use during a conversation. In fact, I hope it is your goal as a teacher for every child in your classroom to be as deeply engaged in conversation with each other as the talking twins are!

## Cultural Differences in How People Converse

Even though the act of conversing is basic to our human nature, what it means to be a *good conversation partner* is not based on an objective standard that is consistent across all groups of people (Collier 1988). In fact, many cultural groups differ in their beliefs about what makes a conversation enjoyable or informative, and on what makes a speaker a good conversation partner. Everyone will approach a conversation from a different perspective because the act of conversing is based on the social rules, cultural values, and communication traditions of people's home language background, their social circles, and their individual personality differences.

Across the globe people can be found conversing, but there will be differences among the many cultures and its individuals. Naturally, one difference is *language.* The *Cambridge Encyclopedia of Language* (Crystal 2010) estimates there are between 3,000 to 10,000 languages currently spoken across the globe. A second difference is the *topic of conversation*: people choose conversation topics based on what is happening in their environments, in social situations, or in their life experiences. Third, there may be differences in *communication style*: for example, in some cultures it may be considered polite to speak softly, while in other cultures some people may use lots of hand gestures, facial expressions, and loud volume. Being aware of differences in communication style is especially important when adults talk about emotional situations with children (Fivush and Wang 2005).

Ultimately, these conversational differences across cultures add to the uniqueness of what makes us all human. But these differences can sometimes cause misunderstanding and miscommunication among us, especially if we're unaware of the variety of conversation skills found in different cultures. One example has already been mentioned: maintaining eye contact holds different significance across cultures. If you try to have a conversation with a child who has been taught *not* to make eye contact with his superiors, you may think the child is being rude or not listening to you even though the child is trying to show you respect and deference. The best thing you as a teacher can do to minimize misunderstanding and miscommunication is to talk with your students' families so that you get to know them and learn more about their home language experiences and traditions.

## Get to Know Your Students' Families

You can make both informal and formal efforts to become familiar with your students' families. Informally, you can take time to chat with family members when they are dropping off or picking up their children. When there are special events going on at school, invite family members personally to come to the event and send invitations home. There are also more formal efforts you can make, such as setting up parent-teacher conferences during convenient times for families to meet you at school. Some programs even ask teachers to do home visits, when the teacher travels to a student's home to visit with the child's family. These kinds of personal visits are often good ways to connect with families. Lastly, another way to get to know families is to ask them to share information about themselves. Below is an example of a survey that asks families about their language-learning activities at home. You can make copies of this version (a template is provided in the appendix) or use it as a starting point to create your own.

# How Is Your Child Talking at Home?

Dear _____ ,

During school, your child will spend a lot of time talking with classmates. I encourage the students to talk about their ideas, opinions, and feelings. I want them to feel free to express themselves. Can you help me learn more about how your child talks at home?

Child's Name: _____ Date of Birth: _____

**Language(s) Spoken at Home**

What language(s) or dialect(s) are spoken in your home? _____

_____

Who speaks to your child in this language(s)/dialect(s)? _____

_____

Do you or a family member ever make up stories and tell them to your child?  ❏ *Yes*  ❏ *No*

Do you or a family member ever tell your child stories about things you did when you were his or her age?

❏ *Yes*  ❏ *No*

Does your child ever make up stories and tell them to you?  ❏ *Yes*  ❏ *No*

Does your child like to be read to?  ❏ *Yes*  ❏ *No*

Does your child pretend to read or try to read when given reading materials?  ❏ *Yes*  ❏ *No*

How many children's books do you have in your house?

*fewer than 10*          *10–20*          *20–40*          *more than 40*

In what language(s) are the children's books?_____

_____

How many times in the past week have you read a storybook to your child?

*Not at all*          *once*          *2–3 times*          *4 or more*

About how old was your child the first time you read to him/her?

*less than 1 yr old*          *1–2 yrs old*          *3–4 yrs old*

## How Is Your Child Talking at Home? (continued)

Do you like to read?    ❑ Yes   ❑ No

In which language(s) do you like to read? _____

_____

What's the name of your child's favorite book? _____

_____

Is your child allowed to use the computer, tablet, e-reader, or smartphone?   ❑ Yes   ❑ No

How many hours per day does your child spend playing on the computer, tablet, e-reader, or smartphone?

_____

How many hours per day does your child spend watching TV? _____

What is your child's favorite TV program? _____

_____

**Bridge from Home to School:**
**Academic Talk Is the Language Used for Classroom Instruction**

At school, teachers use a formal version of English that is considered *academic talk* (van Kleeck 2014). Academic talk follows the grammar and pronunciation rules of Standard English and uses vocabulary terms related to academic subjects like math, science, or reading. For example, you may be leading a discussion about the steps in a math problem and using terms like *subtraction*. Or you might be asking children to make hypotheses as they are conducting science experiments. Even the way teachers talk about stories is different from the way families do at home because teachers will ask children to describe characters or the plot. The vocabulary words involved in these discussions—*experiment*, *test*, *story*, *plot*, and so on—are examples of academic talk.

Many ethnic minority children come to school with limited practice using academic talk because they speak a home language different than the language spoken at school. Some culturally and linguistically diverse (CALD) children may speak Spanish, French, Chinese, Haitian Creole, Jamaican Patois, or an African tribal language. Other children may speak a dialect of English. A dialect is a version of a language that may be used by people from certain social or ethnic groups or geographic regions. One of the most widely used dialects spoken in the United States is African American English (also called African American Vernacular English). Even though children who speak African American English are speaking a version of English, they can still face difficulty during classroom conversations. Some teachers may scold young children for using "broken English" because they do not understand that African American English is a real dialect that has specific grammar, pronunciation, and conversation rules. To learn more about the language features and history of African American English, go to this Public Broadcasting Service (PBS) site: www.pbs.org/speak/education/curriculum/college/aae/.

Whenever you are teaching CALD students, your goal is to create an environment that makes children eager to learn about and practice using academic talk. Use academic talk as a language model for how children should speak at school. Let children know it is okay to speak one language or dialect at school and another language at home. This is called code-switching between a home and school language, and doing so actually helps CALD children's language skills over time. During preschool, children may need time to become familiar with the academic talk at school, so allow children to use their home language or dialect whenever they need to, and never shame them for doing so.

## Get to Know Your Students' (and Your Own) Conversation Styles

Each of us has a unique conversation style. Our conversation styles are based on our personality, our past experiences, our language abilities, and the way we process information. Some of us can be considered more talkative than others, and this is true for children as well as adults.

### Stop and Consider: Your Unique Conversation Style

Learning more about your conversation style can help you better connect with your students. Consider your personal conversation style with the following questions:

Would you describe yourself as a Social Talker, Brief Talker, or Quiet Talker?

_____

In what types of situations or environments do you feel the most talkative? In what types of situations and experiences do you feel like being quieter?

_____

How is your home language tradition different from, or the same as, the "academic talk" language tradition used at school?

_____

_____

What do you enjoy about having conversations with students?

_____

_____

_____

Children are also unique when it comes to their conversation styles (Weitzman and Greenberg 2002). Some children are simply more talkative than others, while others are quieter. The best way to learn about children's conversation styles is to observe them when they are playing and talking with their peers. During typical play interactions with peers, children usually take on one of several conversation styles:

**Social talker:** Children with this style are engaged and talkative with their peers. They regularly initiate and respond to play interactions with their peers. They tend to have speech that is easily understood, and they can verbally express their thoughts, desires, and emotions. They are also good at following the topic of conversations and making comments that are relevant. These children follow the social norms for communicating like using meaningful gestures, making eye contact, and following others' eye gazes and pointing.

**Brief talker:** Children with this style tend to have brief conversations with their peers. Their conversations may be mostly one-sided, without much turn-taking. They may be doing most of the talking but not a lot of listening. They may ignore or reject invitations to play or converse when it doesn't suit their needs. During a conversation, they may only comment on what is relevant to their own desires or perspectives. Even though they don't talk much, they are engaged in the play interaction. When they do talk, their few words are to the point and easily understood.

**Quiet talker:** Children with this style need some time to warm up before they start talking with their peers. They usually do not initiate interactions—instead, they rely on their peers to invite them to play or engage in a group conversation. They may spend most of their time playing alone or not paying attention during a conversation. These children may have speech that is difficult to understand, or they may have a limited vocabulary. They may have difficulty verbally expressing their desires and intentions. These children may be hesitant to speak out in a large group.

It is important to understand children's conversation styles because their styles can affect how you interact with them. For example, you might find yourself spending more time talking with children who are social talkers because they are more likely to come up and talk with you. If you become aware that you are talking to some children more than others, then you should make efforts to talk to those children who are quieter. Another reason it is important to understand children's conversation styles is because these styles affect how they talk to their peers. Later in chapter 3, when I talk about selecting peer group activities, I'll show you how important it is to put children with different conversation styles together in groups.

### The Journey toward Culturally Relevant Instruction

Human beings use language to pass on their culture. You can think of culture and language as the two twisted strands of a rope that are most useful when intertwined. Culturally relevant instruction means teachers intentionally incorporate children's cultural knowledge, traditions, and home language into instructional practices and classroom conversations. Marlene Zepeda, Dina C. Castro, and Sharon Cronin (2011) explain that it is very important for teachers to build upon children's cultural home knowledge because it forms the foundation of their understanding of new content. Children build their knowledge and language skills through interactions with their family and community members. During these home language interactions, they learn the *linguistic code* (such as the words, sentences, or phrases) of their language or dialect. They also learn the *social rules of communication* during home language interactions, such as how to adjust their language based on the listener's knowledge, how to ask questions, and how to tell a story. Children bring these cultural and social rules for communication into the classroom as well, and it is your job to provide instruction that helps them build upon the knowledge they have been developing at home. You can help children build upon their knowledge by engaging in culturally relevant instruction.

## How Can I Become a Good Conversation Partner?

Every teacher can improve her conversation skills by intentionally striving to be a good conversation partner. The fundamentals of being a good conversation partner rest on knowing how to keep a conversation feedback loop going. A feedback loop involves three things: asking open-ended questions, actively listening, and mirroring to expand and clarify what has been said.

First, you *ask open-ended questions* that will spark a dialogue between you and the student. Second, you *actively listen* to what the child has said. You can show that you are actively listening by making eye contact and being genuinely interested and emotionally engaged. Third, after the child has finished responding and you have listened and waited for at least five seconds after the child is done, you *mirror* back what the child has said by repeating, expanding, and clarifying. This feedback loop should be continued throughout the duration of the conversation.

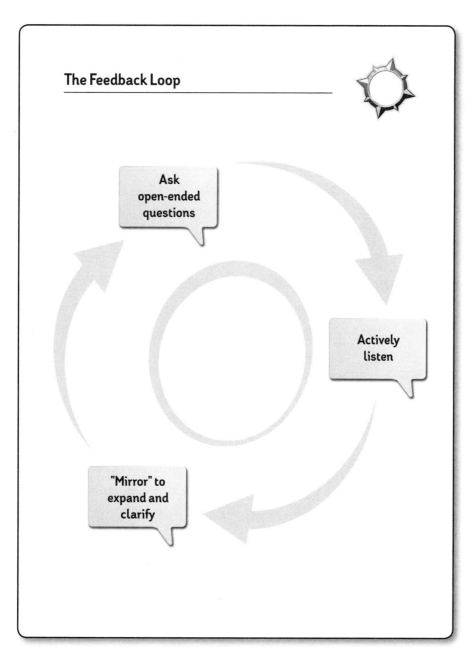

**The Feedback Loop**

Ask open-ended questions

Actively listen

"Mirror" to expand and clarify

A good example of a conversation feedback loop takes place between Miss Rachel and her student Troy. Miss Rachel is having a small-group conversation with her students before they transition to free-choice time. She goes around the table, asking each child what he or she plans to do. She and Troy engage in an extended back-and-forth feedback loop about his plans. Let's break down how Miss Rachel uses the three parts of the feedback loop.

• • •

MISS RACHEL: *What would you like to do for work time today?* [Miss Rachel is asking an open-ended question and then actively listening.]

TROY: *House area.*

MISS RACHEL: *House area? What're you going to do in the house area?* [Miss Rachel asks another open-ended question and continues to actively listen.]

TROY: [Mumbles something about tea.]

MISS RACHEL: *You're going to cook some tea? How're you going to make some tea?* [Miss Rachel asks an open-ended question and actively listens. Then she "mirrors" the open-ended question and listens again.]

TROY: [Mumbles something about coffee.]

MISS RACHEL: *Coffee?* [Miss Rachel mirrors what Troy says in order to clarify.]

TROY: [Mumbles something. This time Miss Rachel can't understand him.]

MISS RACHEL: *But what? Okay. So you're going to make tea or coffee?* [She uses her fingers to count the two choices. Again, she can't understand Troy's answer, but she is trying to clarify using mirroring.]

MISS RACHEL: *Do you want to make tea and coffee? Which one?* [Miss Rachel asks Troy a question to clarify and then listens.]

TROY: *Sugar.*

MISS RACHEL: *Oh, you are going to put sugar in it? And what else are you going put in it?* [Miss Rachel mirrors Troy's response, asks an open-ended question, and listens.]

TROY: *Hot cocoa.*

MISS RACHEL: *Hot cocoa? So it's going to be a mixture of tea and coffee. And you're going to have some sugar in it and hot cocoa? That sounds delicious! Can I have some when you're done?* [Miss Rachel uses mirroring to sum up the conversation and expand on what Troy has said. She ends with a playful open-ended question asking if she can have some of his pretend drink.]

TROY: [Happily nods yes.]

• • •

## Stop and Consider: A Conversation Feedback Loop

Miss Rachel's actions and language, and Troy's responses to her, show that the two were engaged in a successful feedback loop.

List all the questions Miss Rachel used. How many of them were open ended?

_____

_____

_____

_____

How did Miss Rachel show Troy she was listening to him?

_____

_____

_____

How did Miss Rachel handle it when she could not understand Troy?

_____

_____

_____

How do you think Troy felt at the end of the conversation?

_____

_____

_____

## Learn to Use Open-Ended Questions

One of the strengths of Miss Rachel's feedback loop is that she continued to ask Troy open-ended questions. Open-ended questions allow children the opportunity to talk freely and to express their thought processes and opinions. Open-ended questions not only encourage children to talk, but they also foster children's thinking and creativity. Think about open-ended questions as falling into three categories: informing, analyzing, and brainstorming. These categories range in difficulty, depending on the level of creativity and problem solving they address. Usually, information questions are the easiest for children to answer, followed by analyzing and then brainstorming questions.

**Inform:** *Informing* questions focus on details about who, what, when, and where. Teachers rely heavily on these questions because they test students' knowledge about what they have learned. These questions should be used as conversation starting points, not as end points. Informing questions do not drive conceptual development as deeply as the other two categories do.

**Analyze:** *Analyzing* questions, like *how* and *why*, build students' analytical skills. These kinds of questions help students learn to generate explanations for what they have learned, observed, or experienced. These questions work wonders for helping children form their opinions and describe their ideas. These are the types of questions that offer a window into children's minds and thought processes. You should rely heavily on these questions. When you first start to use them, children might hesitate to share their ideas. As you use them more, children will learn that you are interested in their thought process rather than a "correct" answer, and they will become eager to share their ideas and opinions. It will be amazing for you to see how the children blossom into critical thinkers when you use these questions frequently.

**Brainstorm:** *Brainstorming* questions really push children's conceptual development because they encourage children to tap into their creativity. Brainstorming questions ask children to imagine hypothetical situations. These questions force children to speculate about models or explore possibilities instead of just gathering facts or understanding a process. These questions are the root of scientific and artistic thinking and build children's imagination skills!

The question categories build on each other from simple to complex. Together, I call them the Question Trail. The question trail invites children to build their reasoning skills one step at a time.

WHAT DOES IT MEAN TO BE A GOOD CONVERSATION PARTNER?

## The Question Trail

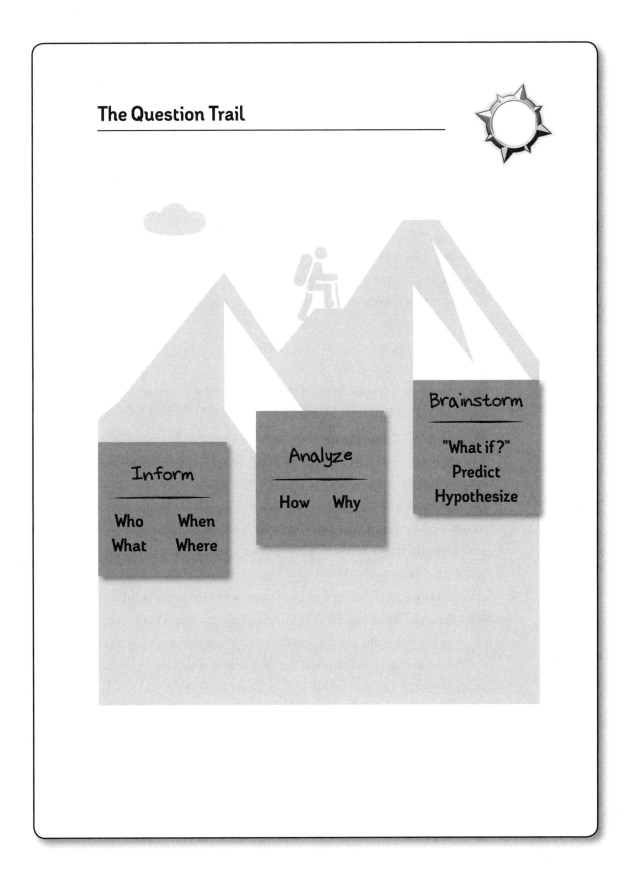

Inform
———
Who    When
What    Where

Analyze
———
How    Why

Brainstorm
———
"What if?"
Predict
Hypothesize

Yes/no questions, on the other hand, have exactly the opposite effect: they stifle communication, thinking, and creativity. Yes/no questions should be used very rarely during instructional conversations.

Sometimes teachers who work with infants or young toddlers and preschoolers with language delays may need to use a yes/no question as an initial starting point to the conversation. If this is necessary, then practice starting with the initial yes/no question and then following up with an Informing question. You might find that many older toddlers, and even preschoolers with language delays, are capable of responding use a few words and meaningful gestures. Once you get into the habit of using the Question Trail, you will use yes/no questions less, and you will find that *all* children's language and cognitive abilities eventually thrive when they are exposed to open-ended questions.

## Learn to Listen

Children are the most important speakers during a conversation! Your job is to *listen* to what children are saying. Listening is a difficult skill to learn. One of the key steps to improving your listening skills is learning to wait before responding. A good rule of thumb is to silently count to five after you ask a question. Remember how one of the hallmarks of good conversation is turn-taking? We all have to learn turn-taking, sometimes even as adults. Practice pausing briefly—just for five seconds—before you take your turn when talking with your students. You will find that within these five seconds, two things may happen. One, the child may say something else, which means you will get even more information about what the child is thinking and feeling. Two, you may have time to think more deeply about what the child has said, and this will help you provide a better response. Think about it: Do you wait a sufficient time for students to answer a question?

Below is an example of a teacher who does not properly use a feedback loop because she fails to listen to what her students are saying.

• • •

*Ms. Madge is seated at the table with a small group of preschoolers who are all fidgeting in their seats. The children have a white card placed in front of each of them. Ms. Madge instructs them to turn the cards over. On each card there is a different shape in a different color.*

MS. MADGE: *Okay, what do we have in front of us?* [She flips over the card in front of her.]

VANESSA: *A square.* [Her card has a blue square on it.]

MS. MADGE: *No. What is it called?*

ESTEBAN: *Triangle.* [His card has a red triangle on it.]

MS. MADGE: *What is this called?* [She points down at her card that has an orange circle on it.]

CAMILLE: *Circle. A circle!*

JAMES: *They're all cards!* [He exclaims, desperately trying to answer Ms. Madge's question.]

MS. MADGE: *No, there's a word for them.*

CAMILLE: *Colors!*

MS. MADGE: *Not colors.*

ESTEBAN: [Mumbles something.]

MS. MADGE: *Shhh! What're they called?*

• • •

## Stop and Consider: Brainstorming How to Strengthen Listening Skills

We can learn a lot from Ms. Madge's example if we think about how she could have done things differently. Take some time to brainstorm how Ms. Madge could strengthen her listening skills.

What could Ms. Madge have done to show she was listening?

_____

_____

_____

_____

Ms. Madge only used informing questions. What are some analyzing and brainstorming questions she could have used?

_____

_____

_____

How do you think the students felt during this conversation?

_____

_____

_____

_____

In this example, Ms. Madge has several opportunities to improve her listening skills. First of all, she fails to realize that her question is unclear. She asks the children what they have in front of them, and three of the children attempt to answer her question with "square," "triangle," and "circle." The children are making honest attempts to engage in a dialogue, but Ms. Madge ignores the fact that they are making good efforts to share their knowledge of shapes and colors. Instead of building on their responses, Ms. Madge is set on getting the children to state a predetermined answer—"shapes." Another problem in this interaction is that the emotional tone is negative. Ms. Madge says "no" repeatedly throughout the conversation. She never offers any praise or encouragement. She even goes so far as to "shhh" a child. In comparison, the previous example with Miss Rachel's conversation with Troy showed a teacher with much better listening skills.

### Learn How to Mirror

Mirroring is an essential part of the feedback loop because it helps the speaker know you understand what he or she is saying. At the beginning of this chapter, I asked you if you had ever had a conversation with someone who misunderstood your point. You probably knew your listener misunderstood because he failed to use any mirroring comments. Perhaps he never repeated or rephrased what you said. Maybe he never asked a clarifying question. Mirroring is especially important to do with young children because sometimes they may not know the exact word or phrase to describe what they are thinking. Children rarely mind when adults mirror their comments. In fact, the more you mirror, the more they keep talking!

## Wrap It Up

The basics of a good conversation are at the heart of our human nature, but we are all unique in our conversation styles because of our home language experiences and cultural backgrounds. As we continue on our journey, keep thinking about how you can use feedback loops to keep conversations going. And consider how open-ended questions build children's reasoning and language skills. By using these simple conversational approaches, you can be intentional about creating a language-learning environment that provides opportunities for children to talk with their peers and for all children to express themselves during group discussions in your classroom.

# Encouraging Instructional Peer Conversations

> Think about a time you heard children problem-solving during a conversation. Did they take turns talking and sharing their ideas? Was a more talkative child taking the lead? How did they manage to resolve any disagreements or misunderstandings?

Children can learn a lot from each other, especially when they are encouraged to share their thoughts and opinions during classroom conversations. The following story is an example of what keen observers children can be and how much they can learn from each other during a conversation.

• • •

*Miss Eileen and her students are huddled around the table. They are engaged in a conversation about the objects pictured in a Pictionary book. The atmosphere is relaxed and nurturing; some children are leaning shoulder to shoulder with their peers, and all the children are attentive and engaged. Miss Eileen explains that she is going to name an object and then the children have to explain either what the object can do or how it can be used.*

MISS EILEEN: *Tree?*

MARIA: *Tree has apple(s).*

MISS EILEEN: *A tree grows fruit. Very good, Maria!*

STEPHEN: *And leaves.*

MISS EILEEN: *Leaves! Uh huh, what else?*

JESSICA: *Umm, they grows.*

MISS EILEEN: *They grow. Yeah!*

BRANDON: *They grow up.*

MISS EILEEN: *Oh boy, that thinking cap is moving!*

BRANDON: *And they grow with seeds.*

MISS EILEEN: *Yeah, they start from a seed.* [She nods her head in agreement.]

KRISTY: *You have to give it some water.*

MISS EILEEN: *You have to water it. What else, Kristy?*

BRANDON: [Mumbles something about trees growing in soil.]

MISS EILEEN: *In soil. Wow!*

• • •

This example shows a teacher engaged in a real-life conversation with her students. Her students are juggling speaking and listening roles, they are building off each other's comments, and they are brainstorming new ideas. Miss Eileen's conversation style might look effortless, but she is intentionally using an *instructional peer conversation* to foster children's skills in critical thinking, collaborative learning, and verbal expression. An instructional peer conversation is a child-led conversation when children work or play together to solve problems, complete an activity, or talk about their experiences, opinions, or ideas. During an instructional peer conversation, teachers have learning objectives for the conversation and use open-ended questions to get children talking.

## Stop and Consider: Understanding Instructional Conversations

Take some time to review what an instructional conversation is. Test your knowledge by answering the questions below.

**In your own words, describe what a peer instructional conversation is.**

_____

_____

_____

_____

_____

**Circle all the things children might do during an instructional conversation.**

work or play together to solve problems          talk about their experiences, opinion, or ideas

complete an activity          listen to the teacher read a story

**Fill in the blank.**

During instructional peer conversations, teachers create _____

and _____

to encourage children to talk.

*Answers to fill-in-the-blank:* learning objectives; open-ended questions.

# Why Are Peer Conversations Important?

If I ask you to imagine a typical conversation in the classroom, you may picture a teacher talking with a group of students about a learning activity. For example, you may imagine a teacher engaging children in a conversation about why ice cubes melt in warm water. This type of discussion usually happens just once or twice a day, maybe during circle time or a specific small-group learning activity. But children have many conversations throughout the day with their peers!

## Peer Conversations Happen a Lot

Lots of opportunities arise throughout the day for children to engage in peer discussions, and these discussions are meaningful and important—just as important as teacher-led group discussions. What researchers find most often when they examine classroom conversations is that children spend the majority of their time throughout the day talking to their peers, not the teacher. Dickinson (2001) reports that whole-group discussions, such as circle time, only happen for a very small portion of the day. When Early and her colleagues (2010) investigated over 400 early education classrooms across several states, they found that children spent 29 percent of their day in free-choice, child-led activities like center play with peers. Children also spent another 34 percent of their time in classroom routines like meal times, cleanup, or transitions. Children spent the remaining 37 percent of their time in teacher-assigned activities in which small groups of children were assigned to work together. In real-life classrooms, children actually spend most of their school day talking to each other, either during peer play or small group activities.

## Peer Conversations Foster Social Skills

Peer interaction is important to children's learning and growth in their social skills. Talking with peers provides the social opportunity to communicate with equals— when children talk with each other, they are more likely to express their opinions and have disagreements. Developing the ability to navigate a disagreement with a peer is a valuable skill for young children to learn, and it can only be learned through trial and error. So whenever it is safe and appropriate, encourage children to talk through their differing points of view.

## Peer Conversations Boost Language Development

Children's peers are also good language partners because they can boost each other's language development. Research studies show how essential peers are as language partners for young children, especially those who are less talkative. For instance, several studies have found that children with lower language abilities benefit from being in classrooms with peers who have strong language and reading skills (Henry and Rickman 2007; Justice et al. 2011; Schechter and Bye 2007). When children who are more talkative play with children who are less talkative, the talkative peer elevates the conversation, adding vocabulary, grammar, and new ideas.

In the following example, Gabriella brings new ideas and language to the play interaction between Belita and Claudia. All of the girls in this example are culturally and linguistically diverse learners.

● ● ●

*Belita and Claudia are seated in the block area, playing with cars.*

BELITA: *Me sito.*

CLAUDIA [crawling on the floor, pushing a toy]: *Beep, beep, beep!*

BELITA [motioning to Claudia to sit down]: *Yeah, yeah, yeah, yeah.*

CLAUDIA: *Beep, beep! Belita. Agh! What?*

BELITA [also pushing a car]: *Beep, beep, beep!*

GABRIELLA [approaching the girls with a big smile]: *Look, girls, it's me!*

BELITA: *Beep, beep!*

CLAUDIA: *Beep, beep!*

GABRIELLA: *It's me!*

CLAUDIA [passing Gabriella a truck]: *Here you go.*

GABRIELLA [driving the cars into a tower of blocks]: *Beep! Beep, beep. Ah, start looking here. Bombs away!*

BELITA: *Ow!*

CLAUDIA: *Gabriella! Gabriella!*

GABRIELLA: *Is it an awesome good idea?*

CLAUDIA: *Yes! It's a good idea!*

BELITA: *Beep!*

GABRIELLA: *Isn't it?*

CLAUDIA: *Good idea!*

BELITA: *Oh yeah!*

CLAUDIA [points to a set of blocks]: *Whoa! Wait. Those, Gabriella.*

GABRIELLA [searching for the final block to put at the top of their tower]: *Where was the last one?*

CLAUDIA: *Go! Go!*

BELITA [laughing]: *Yeah, go!*

• • •

The girls in this interaction have different language abilities. Belita mostly uses the same words throughout the interaction, but she does begin the interaction using some language mixing: "Me sito" is a conjugation of the English verb "to sit" into a Spanish reflexive grammatical form (*sentarse*). (Displaying this language mixing is actually a positive sign of *advancement* in language skills because it shows that Belita understands that languages have grammatical rules and she is practicing applying these rules.) Gabriella brings some new vocabulary words into the dialogue and a new play idea of crashing cars into the block tower, and all three girls are excited and engaged.

## Peer Conversations Model Language

When children with lower language abilities interact with more talkative peers, they learn to conform to the *peer language model*. Peers model language for each other by providing examples of speech (and even writing) that are socially acceptable within their age or social group. It's natural to conform to the way of speaking of those around us. Young children are no different. In fact, they are even more influenced by peer language models than older children because young children often adopt the communication patterns of those around them quickly, easily, and without intentional effort. Also, peers can help those with lower language abilities develop *meta-linguistic awareness*, or the ability to critically think about the features of language and evaluate what has been said.

One way that peers model language is by introducing new words and terms. Preschool children ages two to five are going through a period of language vocabulary development known as *fast mapping*, which is a stage in which they can quickly and quite accurately pick up new vocabulary terms. Children are constantly learning new words and expressions from each other. Have you ever asked a child, "Where did you learn that word?" only to find out that a friend at school used it? It may even be easier for children than adults to learn words from each other because they usually do so during emotional interactions, whether positive (such as having fun during joint play) or negative (such as during teasing or bullying).

Another way peers model language is by "filling in the blanks." Sometimes a talkative child can ease the burden of communication by helping a quieter child articulate what he wants to say or even by correcting him. Take, for example, this dialogue between a teacher and two students about coloring.

• • •

TEACHER: *Diana, what news do you have for us today?*

DIANA: *I colored in my house.*

TEACHER: *You were coloring in your house? What did you color?*

DIANA: *Red, brown, purple, orange, and black.*

TEACHER: *Red, brown, purple, orange, and black?*

DIANA: *Yes.*

KENNETH: *And yellow.*

TEACHER: *Diana didn't say yellow. You were helping her, Kenneth.*

• • •

Kenneth's comment adds more information about Diana's experience. In this way, children can aid their peers' language development even through comments in conversation.

## Bridge from Home to School:
## How Peers Can Support the Communication Skills of CALD Learners

Peers play a critical role in building the language skills of culturally and linguistically diverse (CALD) learners, so make special efforts to incorporate language-minority children into the peer interactions of the class. Here are several things you can do to ensure that CALD children feel welcome and are well received by their peers.

**Build children's curiosity about languages.** This is the most important intentional effort you can make to ensure CALD children are well received by their peers. Build the monolingual English children's curiosity by introducing them to the concept of different languages. Lead the class in discussions about how people may speak different languages at home. Be sure to emphasize that it is a good thing to speak multiple languages.

**Use children's home language(s).** Incorporate fun new words from a CALD child's home language into the classroom. Read books or sing songs during circle time that have words from the home language. You might also introduce computer games or books on tape that show children who are using two languages and code-switching between their home language/dialect and academic talk.

**Create a positive perception of the CALD learner.** Even young children can have negative perceptions and stereotypes about peers who speak differently. It is important for you to actively try to *change children's perceptions* of CALD speakers and what they can do. Many games children play together actually require a good bit of language comprehension and production, so children with limited or different language skills may not be popular playmates. For example, children who are frustrated by a peer with limited language skills often complain, "She can't say anything . . ." or "He doesn't know how to play properly" (Weitzman and Greenberg 2002, 215). You can respond by saying, "There are so many games you could play with [her] that don't need talking . . . She loves running games and playing with 'goop.' I'll bet you could think of some games you could play with her, and you can let me know if you need anything for them" (Weitzman and Greenberg 2002, 215).

**Model good communication skills.** When talking with CALD children, model your responses for other children. Show them how to listen carefully when talking to their CALD peers, and encourage all children to feel free to use meaningful gestures (like pointing) and big facial expressions when talking to each other. Use these gestures and expressions yourself when you talk to CALD students, and include them in your group.

## How Do You Foster Peer Conversations?

On a daily basis, it's rare for a teacher to sit down one-on-one and engage in an extended conversation with each and every child. One-on-one conversations are also rare because children typically end up talking in groups, usually of two to four children, while they engage in group work or play activities. In early childhood classrooms, almost all conversations have multiple peers engaged because children eagerly chime in when the teacher is talking to a single child or when their peers are talking to each other. You can maximize on these naturally occurring peer discussions by learning a few techniques. Intentionally directing questions to the group rather than individual children and showing them how to model questions helps children learn how to foster conversations with each other.

## Stop and Consider: How Do You Encourage Peer Conversations?

Sometimes the way we ask questions lets children know that it's okay for them to talk to the peers group when responding during a conversation. Think about how you encourage children to have peer conversations.

During a group conversation, do you direct questions to individual children? Or do you direct them to the group so that children know everyone is free to answer?

_____

_____

_____

How can you encourage students to speak to each other when responding to questions?

_____

_____

_____

How can you model children asking each other questions?

_____

_____

_____

What opportunities do you provide for children to ask each other questions?

_____

_____

_____

## Learn How to Juggle a Peer Conversation

Many teachers handle classroom conversations by tightening control over the dialogue. Tightening control over the conversation—such as by calling on individual children or by asking yes/no questions—can limit classroom dialogue. By calling on children, you control which children speak. This method can be stifling to talkative children, whose natural tendency is to chime in to the conversation whenever they have something to say. Similarly, when you ask yes/no questions, you are asking for a response from children but only requiring children to agree or disagree with what is being said. The challenge you face is learning how to juggle a peer conversation. When you juggle a peer conversation, you empower your students by sharing control of the conversation with them. When you juggle a conversation, you allow students to speak more and follow their natural tendencies. The strategies you use to juggle conversations have the goal of getting the children to talk more than you. In order to do this, you have to intentionally plan how to ask questions and provide feedback. Here are some suggestions for how you can juggle a peer conversation:

- Allow children to call on each other ("Pick one of your friends who has a question").

- Provide a speaking prop (for instance, toy, stick, ball) that is passed around and provides a tactile, hands-on reminder of whose turn it is to speak.

- Pose questions to the group rather than to individual children. Ask open-ended questions and encourage children to do the same.

- Encourage children to answer each other's questions.

- Deflect the conversation away from yourself by referring back to what children have said.

## Foster Small-Group Work Activities

Small-group work is another ideal place for children to engage in peer discussions. Unlike in their play interactions, children do not naturally form small working groups. These groups are teacher assigned, so they are the perfect place for you to plan for some instructional peer conversations. When setting up these small groups, you should aim at the ideal group size of two to four children. This small group size ensures that quieter children have the opportunity to participate in the conversation. In fact, it is even better to limit the group size to two, if one child is really quiet.

When you pick an activity, think about how it can support children's critical thinking, planning, and language skills to solve a problem together. Below are examples of small-group work activities that can foster children's conversation skills. These activities can be used and adapted to meet a variety of conversational goals.

## ACTIVITY

## Make Small Talk

Encourage children to share information about their past experiences, ideas, and opinions. Research by McCabe and Bliss (2002) shows that simple, open-ended conversation starters like "Have you ever been to the beach? Tell me what happened when you visited there" are enough to get children talking about their life experiences. Planning time for children to engage in this type of small talk helps children build their language and social skills.

Seat two to four children together in a quiet area of the classroom and present them with a "Have you ever . . ." topic. Be sure to choose a common experience that you know most children have had, like going to the dentist, getting a shot, or helping their mom cook dinner. Encourage the other children to ask follow-up questions, like *What happened? What did you do? Why did you do that? How did you feel?* Once you see that children have gotten the hang of asking each other questions to get more details, then slip into the background and let them do the talking and questioning. Once each child has participated in a small group, you can then have a larger discussion with the whole group, asking children to share what they learned about their friends' past experiences.

## Conduct Interviews

Teach children how to use conversations to collect information. Work with a small group of two to four children seated at a table in a quiet area of the classroom. At the top of a piece of large paper, write a Yes/No question, such as *Do you have a pet? Do you have a sibling?* (In this activity, a Yes/No question is appropriate because you want to help children gather some simple data.) Leave space on the paper for children to write their names and their answers to the question. The page might look something like this:

Question: Do you have a pet?

| | Yes | No |
|---|---|---|
| Isaac | ✔ | |
| Troy | | ✔ |
| Michelle | ✔ | |

Have the children use their emergent writing skills to write their names and to check off their answers to the question. After the children have recorded their answers, ask them analyzing questions (*How many of you have pets?*) and informing questions (*What are the names of your pets? What kind of pet is it?*). Prompt them to ask each other questions about the data. (Let's think about some questions we can ask our friends about their pets. Could we ask our friends what kinds of pets they have? Or what about their pets' names? What else might we want to know about our friends' pets?) Once everyone has answered the question in his or her small group, you can take the data chart and share it with the whole class and begin a discussion with the group around how many children have pets or what they like about their pets.

ACTIVITY

## Book Club Meeting

Invite two to four children to sit together to discuss a story that you have recently read to the class. For example, you might choose the story that you read at circle time. Place a copy of the book with the children so that they can look at the pages and refresh their memories if they need to. Encourage them to have a conversation about the important elements of the story. Good questions to ask might be *Who is the main character? What is the story about? How did the story end?* You can also encourage children to share their opinion about the story: *Did you like it?* After everyone has participated in the book club meeting, you can talk about the book again with the larger group. Again, asking children to share their favorite parts of the story and main characters.

ACTIVITY

## Peacemaking Murals

Allow two to four children to brainstorm about social problems they encounter in the classroom, such as teasing or not sharing. Present the problem to the group and ask them to think about what they could do to solve it. Line a small table with a big piece of mural paper and write a question in the center of the paper, like "What Can We Do to Stop Teasing?" or "Why Is it Important to Share?" Have children brainstorm ideas and then draw pictures of their ideas. Then have them add to each other's ideas. (Eric says that we can use nice words to stop teasing. Nico, can you help Eric think of some nice words to use that might stop teasing?) Once everyone in the group has had the chance to participate in a small-group peacemaking discussion, then you can hang the mural and talk about all the ideas the children came up with to solve the problem.

## Playwriting

ACTIVITY

For this activity, take a large piece of paper and divide it into three sections that you will label *Beginning*, *Middle*, and *End*. Ask a small group of two to four children to make up a "play," and explain to them that a play is a story that they will act out in front of the class. Remind the children that they have to make up the play together. So pose questions to the group like, "What do you all want your story to be about?" Let the children brainstorm for a minute. Once they have agreed on a topic, ask them to describe what happens in the beginning, middle, and end of their play. Tell the children they have to decide who is going to draw the pictures for each "scene" (beginning, middle, and end) and who is going to act out those parts. Once the children have created their play, allow them to act it out during a whole group discussion time. After the children have acted out their play, lead the whole group in a discussion about what happened in the play and who the characters were.

## Foster Peer Play

Most early childhood curricula schedule time in the day for free-play or center-choice activities. Play provides an opportunity for children to really take the lead during interactions. Researchers have found that teachers are less likely to dominate conversations when children are playing together (Gest et al. 2006). Teachers usually stand on the outskirts of play and let children set the tone and direction for their conversations during play. Play is when children are in charge!

Teachers can maximize on these free-play times by ensuring that *all* children are equally involved in group play. If you understand why some children are being excluded, you'll be better able to make sure all children are included. One reason children can be left out of play is that their social skills are not as well developed as their peers'; for instance, some children may lack the confidence to initiate peer interactions. Teachers can help those children learn how to enter into the play. To do so, you can model for them how to initiate invitations to play. For example, you might bring John and Sara face-to-face and say, "Why don't you guys play in the block area together?" Another reason children may be excluded from play groups is that their language skills are less developed. Children with limited language abilities may struggle to understand what others are saying to them, or others may misunderstand their efforts to express themselves. As a teacher, you can provide support for such children by modeling language for them to repeat ("John, how about you ask Sara if she wants to play with the blocks?"). Helping all children to be included may just involve a little outside guidance.

Below is an example of a child who is having difficulty entering into a play interaction during free-choice time. As you read the example, think about what the teacher could have done to help bridge the gap between the two children and encourage them to play together.

• • •

*Ariana is playing in the house area, pretending to cook dinner. She bustles around, placing dishes and pretend food on the table. Lucas approaches with a smile and starts to speak to her in Chinese. Ariana looks puzzled because she doesn't speak Chinese, then tells him, "You need to use your words."*

• • •

## Stop and Consider: Fostering Friendships among Children Who Speak Different Languages

In the preceding story, Lucas, a newly enrolled Chinese-speaking child, tried to initiate a peer conversation with Ariana, a talkative monolingual English speaker. Because Ariana did not speak Chinese, the interaction was stifled, possibly leaving both of them confused and Lucas feeling rejected.

What could a teacher do to facilitate an interaction between the two children?

_____

_____

_____

_____

How might a teacher educate Ariana about the language Lucas speaks?

_____

_____

_____

_____

How could a teacher encourage a friendship between the two children?

_____

_____

_____

_____

Like small-group work activities, peer-play interactions can be used to foster children's critical thinking and collaborative learning. Play activities are not as dependent on the use of open-ended questions as small group work activities are. Instead, the goal of play interactions is to get children talking to each other and to make sure that all children are involved in these high-level play activities. Below are some suggestions for play activities that can get children talking and can be adapted to a variety of conversational goals.

Small-group work and peer-play activities serve as ways for you to help peers start conversations with each other. These activities can be used again and again. In fact, children get better at them the more they are exposed to them. You can use these activities when you plan peer instructional conversations. These activities form the basis for what children *do* and *talk about* during their conversations with each other.

---

**ACTIVITY**

## "Thematic" Pretend Play

The goal for this peer play activity is simply to get children talking to each other and engaged in meaningful conversations about these pretend scenarios. Limit the group to two to four children so that each child has the opportunity to meaningfully contribute to the dialogue. (Sometimes quiet children can get lost in the shuffle when there are too many children involved in a pretend play scenario.) Incorporate "themes" into children's sociodrama so that children can become more creative with their pretend play scenarios. For example, set up an area of the room as a post office, restaurant, doctor's office, or cyber cafe. Arrange this area so that it has materials that would common in these locations, such as envelopes, stamps, menus, coffee mugs, computers, and stethoscopes. The possibilities for places and props are endless. Be creative!

## Scavenger Hunt

The goal for this activity is to get the children to work collaboratively toward a common goal. Group two to four children together and set them out on a task to find certain objects around the room. This is an activity that can be done with many groups simultaneously, and each group may have a slightly different object to find. For example, one group may have to find five blue objects in the room, while another has to find five yellow ones. Or one group may have to find large items while another finds tiny items. Make sure the children understand that they have to work as a team. They must search and find the objects together. Be sure to give each group a bag or basket to gather the items in.

## Wrap It Up

Since children spend so much time talking with each other throughout the day, you have many opportunities to help them foster instructional peer conversations. Not only do instructional peer conversations build children's critical-thinking skills and collaborative learning, but they also foster friendship and social skills. Look for opportunities to plan activities where peers can talk to each other.

# Planning Instructional Peer Conversations

What was the best classroom conversation you recently had with a group of students? What was the conversation about? Were the children listening and talking to each other? What do you think the children learned from each other?

Often in early childhood classrooms, children approach teachers and start a conversation about whatever is on their minds. Your job in this situation is to ensure that the conversation continues by engaging the children in a conversation feedback loop. These spontaneous, child-initiated conversations require no planning on your part.

An *instructional* peer conversation, on the other hand, takes some special effort from you. You'll need to plan where you want the conversation to go and how you want to get there. The Conversation Compass approach includes two tools that can help you map out your conversation plans: The compass itself is a visual tool that reminds you of the key elements of the approach. The map is a write-in tool that guides you through the three important steps in instructional peer conversation planning:

1. Set up peer groups in an activity (such as those described in chapter 2) to encourage collaborative learning and dialogue among peers.

2. Choose which conceptual reasoning skills—literacy, math, reading, or science—you will target to guide children's thinking and academic talk.

3. Map out open-ended questions (using the question trail from chapter 1) to drive concept development and engage children in meaningful dialogue with their peers.

### Children Are in Control During the Small-Group Peer Conversations

A word of caution: instructional peer conversations are *not* a time for you to be in control. Even though you have planned for ways to introduce concepts and open-ended questions during group activities, you should still follow the children's lead and allow them to set the pace of the conversation. In fact, once children get into the habit of engaging in these small group conversations, they will be able to talk and problem solve with each other with only limited input from you. Let the children take the driver's seat!

When planning an instructional peer conversation, think about how you are going to encourage children to talk more and cooperate during problem solving.

Children are able to really demonstrate their abilities when teachers engage them in planned instructional conversations. When I think about conversations I have had with children, I'm always reminded of what astute observers they can be and how much they delight in sharing their ideas and observations, especially when given the opportunity to talk with their peers.

## Stop and Consider: How Do You Plan for Conversations Now?

Take some time to think about the activities and tools you are now using to foster conversations.

What steps do you take to plan for small groups of children to have peer conversations?

_____

_____

_____

_____

What types of activities do you use to engage children in group conversations? How do you tie these activities to literacy, math, science, or social-emotional development?

_____

_____

_____

_____

How do you choose the open-ended questions you ask children during the activity? Do you select these questions beforehand?

_____

_____

_____

_____

# Why Should You Plan Instructional Peer Conversations?

Peer conversations naturally provide children with the opportunity to learn from their peers. With a little help from you, children's conversations can go even further. When you plan instructional conversations, you scaffold children's dialogue by setting up activities, learning goals, and questions that encourage children to think critically and express their ideas. Planned instructional peer conversations can promote academic reasoning and academic talk.

## Instructional Peer Conversations Promote Reasoning about Academic Concepts

Child development and cognitive-learning theories demonstrate that people understand information better when it is presented in conversations instead of lectures (Garrod and Pickering 2004; Chapman 2000; Halliday 2004; Rogoff 1994). In lectures the roles of speaker and listener are set, but in conversations the roles alternate. During conversations both the speaker and listener are cooperatively involved in constructing the *meaning* of what is being said. The cooperative meaning-making that occurs during conversations is what drives conceptual reasoning. Children's conceptual development includes practicing many thinking and reasoning skills:

- problem solving
- predicting
- classifying
- comparing
- planning
- evaluating
- brainstorming
- integrating
- reminiscing
- making real-world connections
- explaining thoughts and ideas

All of these skills are critical for academic success. Children need many opportunities to practice them in the classroom. Consider focusing on skills like these when planning conversations to build children's conceptual reasoning. Below is an example in which Miss Aneta has planned a conversation about science, and she comes prepared for the conversation with pictures of hibernating animals.

• • •

*Miss Aneta is seated on the carpet with a small group of preschoolers circled around her. The students in her classroom are ethnically diverse, and they come from a variety of home language backgrounds. Pinned on the wall behind Miss Aneta are pictures and messages written in English and Spanish. The children are talking about hibernation. Each time a child names an animal that hibernates, Miss Aneta writes the name on the whiteboard and tapes a picture of the animal next to the name. After the children have generated a list, she asks them to pick an animal and pretend to hibernate like that animal. The children get excited as they take positions on the floor, pretending to sleep like bears or bats or wood frogs.*

• • •

### Stop and Consider: What Background Work Is Needed Before Planning a Conversation?

Think about the steps Miss Aneta had to take to plan for this conversation.

What materials did she need to print out and have ready to use beforehand?

_____

_____

What information did Miss Aneta have to investigate before she could lead the children in this discussion?

_____

_____

How did she make efforts to ensure that culturally and linguistically diverse (CALD) students could follow the conversation?

_____

_____

One of the great things Miss Aneta did was to try to boost the CALD children's vocabulary. She knew that seeing the pictures would expand the children's understanding because it would link new vocabulary terms to visual images. Miss Aneta knew that linking visuals and words is an important strategy to build any children's vocabulary, but this strategy is especially important when teaching children who may speak a home language different from the language spoken at school. Exposing children to new vocabulary words, especially those related to science and math, is key to fostering their academic talk.

## Instructional Peer Conversations Let Children Practice Using Academic Talk

To be successful communicators at school, children need to be able to explain their ideas and feelings in a way that others can understand clearly. In order to do this, they need to know the words to describe what they are talking about. In essence, children need to be able to use the *academic talk* discussed in chapter 1. Teachers use academic talk to instruct students and help them develop abstract reasoning, new vocabulary, and critical-thinking skills. Miss Aneta used academic talk to teach the children new, science-related vocabulary terms like *hibernation* and *wood frog*.

Giving preschoolers the chance to practice using academic talk lays the foundation for the literacy, math, and science skills they will need in kindergarten and beyond. In fact, the *Common Core Standards for English Language Arts and Literacy* (www.corestandards.org/ELA-Literacy/SL/K/) affirms that kindergartners need to be able to use academic talk to engage in collaborative conversations with diverse peers. The standards say that children should be able to express knowledge and ideas clearly and to pick up new vocabulary words. But engaging in academic talk is about more than just learning new vocabulary. It is also about being able to use that vocabulary to generate and classify ideas, as in answering questions like "Which animals hibernate during winter?" You can encourage preschoolers' use of academic talk by engaging them in conversations about letters, numbers, logos and icons, maps, and vocabulary words, or by giving them time to engage in pretend play.

## Planning Tool: Use the Compass to Guide Academic Reasoning and Talk

Think about what the learning objective is for your conversation. What reasoning skills do you want the children to practice during a group activity? The compass is designed to help you visualize and plan the academic reasoning path you'll take with the children. The compass's reasoning paths focus on key academic skills children will encounter in kindergarten: literacy reasoning, science reasoning, math reasoning, and social reasoning. The reasoning paths can help you organize what you'd like children to learn during their discussions. Adjacent to the reasoning paths are suggestions for small-group and play activities, which are described in chapter 2—these are ideal for jump-starting topics for conversation. You can easily adapt most activities to any reasoning path. Then you can create a question trail for the activity and reasoning path you've chosen.

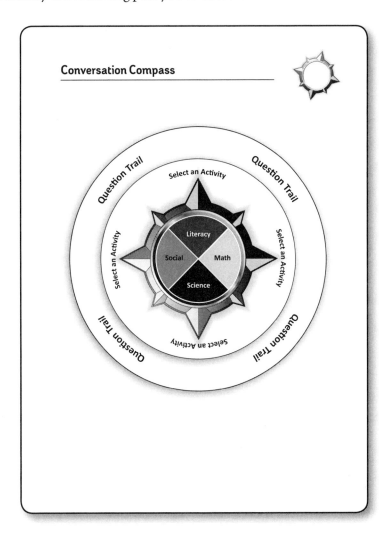

**Literacy path:** The literacy reasoning path focuses on building skills that are related to future reading skills. This path emphasizes vocabulary skills, such as children's ability to define a word or concept by explaining the meaning of a word, symbol, or picture. This path also focuses on building children's understanding of literature by asking them to talk about the structure of a story (that is, what happens at the beginning, middle, and end) or to discuss what information the author is trying to convey in an expository text. For example, in a book about skeletons, you might engage children in a conversation about all the new things they have learned about bones. Lastly, this path focuses on developing print skills by allowing children to talk about letters and the sounds letters make (this is called *phonemic awareness*).

**Science path:** The science reasoning path develops children's observation, planning, and scientific inquiry skills. It also focuses on helping children learn how to problem solve and brainstorm alternative solutions. This path also helps them to hypothesize—that is, to develop their abilities to predict what might happen in the future. For example, one possible discussion along the science-reasoning path could ask children to problem solve by describing alternative solutions to a problem or the steps or methods for a plan. Another possible conversation could ask children to predict the future or make "if/then" guesses about cause-and-effect situations.

**Math path:** The math reasoning path develops children's ability to compare and contrast and understand how to systematically gather information. This path also focuses on children's understanding of numbers, geometric shapes, algebraic concepts like patterns and sequencing, and statistical concepts like probability. You can introduce some important math skills by having children collect, report, and analyze data. The Conducting Interviews peer activity (chapter 2) is an example of the math reasoning path. After conducting interviews, children can discuss the data they recorded and summarize their results. These activities help build later math skills.

**Social path:** The social reasoning path emphasizes children's ability to talk about past experiences or explain their thoughts, feelings, desires, and motivations. This path also focuses on their abilities to use their imaginations to talk about pretend-play experiences or fantasy situations. Even though social reasoning is not a traditional academic skill, it is still extremely important for children's school success. Children who have positive social skills get along with their peers better and form stronger ties with their teachers. Discussions along this reasoning path could be inspired by activities like Make Small Talk and Peacemaking Murals discussed in chapter 2.

## How Do You Plan a Peer Instructional Conversation?

In classrooms with high-quality language learning environments, teachers are intentional about how they talk to children. Research shows that teachers' conversations are better when they intentionally use language-based lesson planning materials and engage children in play-based language activities (Cabell et al. 2011; Justice et al. 2008; Piasta et al. 2012; Connor et al. 2006). Teachers can plan conversations as a part of their daily routine.

### When You Don't Plan, Prepare for the Worst

Perhaps the best way to see the usefulness of planning an instructional conversation is to observe what can happen when a teacher does not plan.

● ● ●

*Miss Stacey is leading a counting activity with a small group of students, but she is distracted by what is happening across the room. Many of the children are also looking across the room. Only the two girls seated closest to her are paying attention. Miss Stacey is asking the children to roll dice, count the number of dots, and then tell her what they did during free-choice time.*

MISS STACEY: *Okay, give it to Katie.* [A child passes the dice to Katie]. *Okay, throw it.* [Katie rolls the dice.]

MISS STACEY: *What did you get?*

KATIE: *One, two, three, four.*

MISS STACEY: *Okay, where did you work today?*

KATIE: *I worked with the marbles.*

MISS STACEY: *Where did you work?* [She is distracted because her co-teacher is talking to her.]

KATIE: [Katie repeats herself.] *I worked with the marbles.*

MISS STACEY: *Stay over here.* [She says to child in lap.]

KATIE: *I build a house in the block area.*

MISS STACEY: *Played in the block area? Give it to Tiffany.* [Katie passes the dice to Tiffany.] *Tiffany, roll the dice.* [Tiffany rolls dice, but Miss Stacey is looking away and doesn't notice. Still looking across the room, she directs the child again.] *Tiffany, roll the dice.*

[Tiffany rolls dice second time and starts to count.]

MISS STACEY: *Tiffany, roll the dice.* [Child rolls dice a third time, and the teacher finally notices.]

MISS STACEY: *Okay, now how many?*

TIFFANY: *Two.*

MISS STACEY: *Two. Okay, where did you work? Tiffany, where did you work?*

TIFFANY: *In the sand area.*

MISS STACEY: *Played in the sand area today?* [Tiffany nods.] *Okay, hand it to Lisa.*

• • •

Let's think about how Miss Stacey's conversation strays from the three steps to planning an instructional peer conversation.

**1. Set up peer groups and a learning activity.** The activity Miss Stacey chose was not well suited to fostering conversations. Children had to wait their turn to roll the dice before they could speak. Activities like this stop the flow of the conversation because children can't talk freely. This type of activity also doesn't build collaborative learning. The children didn't have the opportunity to engage in meaning-making because there was no problem to be solved and no true conversation topic. The small-group work and play activities described in chapter 2 (see pages 38–45) are better suited to support children's free-flowing dialogue in which they can solve a problem or discuss a topic.

**2. Choose compass reasoning skills to target.** Miss Stacey's conversation could have promoted higher-order reasoning by asking children to recall and describe their activities during free-choice. Instead, the conversation was bogged down by Miss Stacey's management of rolling the dice, getting a child to stay seated, and distractions across the room. It's not clear that Miss Stacey was truly trying to teach the children anything. Instead, it seems as though she was simply going through the motions and not really paying attention. For example, when it was Tiffany's turn to roll the dice, Miss Stacey was so distracted that she didn't even notice. The social reasoning path would have suited this conversation well. That path focuses on allowing children to reminisce, connect, and share their past experiences.

**3. Map out open-ended questions.** Remember the feedback loop in chapter 1 (see page 17)? The way to keep a conversation going is by asking open-ended questions, but these questions must come in a cycle that also includes active listening and mirroring. One positive aspect of Miss Stacey's conversation is that she mirrored or repeated back what the children said. Unfortunately, she rarely made eye contact as she mirrored, which may have led the children to wonder if she was truly listening and interested in what they said. Miss Stacey did ask an open-ended question: "Where did you work today?" But she asked the same question to all the children after they rolled the dice, and she never asked any follow-up questions about what the children did. Using questions in this way sets up a hierarchy in which only Miss Stacey has the power to ask the questions. She set up the expectation that, as teacher, she would ask a set question, and each student was expected to give her a brief answer—no elaboration, no discussion. This type of questioning is not part of the Conversation Compass approach. The goal of open-ended questions is to keep the feedback loop going.

## Planning Tool: Use the Map to Plan a Conversation

So what can you do to avoid a conversation meltdown? The map is a tool to help you think about, structure, and plan instructional peer conversations before they happen. Using the map will help you avoid some of the mistakes Miss Stacey made. The more you use the map, the better you will become at leading instructional peer conversations. And the better children will become at engaging in these conversations! Let's walk through a step-by-step example of how you can create a map to plan a peer conversation.

**Step 1: Set up peer groups and a learning activity**

Assign peer groups of two to four children to work together during an activity, being sure that the peer groupings are a mixture of talkative versus quiet children and CALD children. For this example, you might decide to use the Scavenger Hunt peer-play activity. (The peer-group activities in chapter 2 offer suggestions for activities to get children talking. You can use the compass and the map with almost any type of activity.) The activity you choose should last no longer than ten to fifteen minutes, so children won't become bored or distracted.

Before you start a peer instructional conversation, introduce the activity and give children specific instructions about what they will do. For this example, you can break down the Scavenger Hunt like this:

1.  Tell the children they will work in small groups to look for objects around the room.

2.  Tell them they will sort the objects into boxes labeled *large*, *medium*, and *small*.

3.  Tell them that at the end of their hunt, they will talk about what they found with the larger class and count the number of objects by size.

## The Conversation Map

*Use this form to plan your instructional peer conversation. Follow each step and write down your plan.*

• • • • • • •

**Step 1:** Select and explain the activity and set up the peer groups (2–4 children).

**Activity:**  Scavenger Hunt

| Group 1 | Group 2 | Group 3 | Group 4 | Group 5 | Group 6 |
|---------|---------|---------|---------|---------|---------|
| Eric | Isaac | Makaylah | Lucas | Juan | Derreck |
| Belita | Xavier | Sasha | Michelle | Jose | Rachel |
| Ariana | Warren | Shemeca | Yanique | Amina | Meena |
| | | | | | |

**Step 2: Choose a Compass Reasoning Path**

Think about what you want children to learn from the activity. Which conceptual reasoning path do you want to explore during the conversation? In our example, the Scavenger Hunt activity lends itself well to conversations around math reasoning. But this same activity might be used to inspire conversations about science reasoning if children are looking for objects in nature, or even literacy, if you have the children search for objects that begin with a certain letter. If you are creative, you will find that all the activities can be used with any of the reasoning paths.

For this example, you will ask children to find objects of varying sizes, so you select the math reasoning path. This activity fits nicely with the math reasoning path because children have to think about objects' dimensions, compare and contrast objects of different sizes, and then summarize what they have learned from the data. As children search for the items, they naturally begin to engage in conversations with each other to discuss which items are the appropriate sizes. They also have to collaborate and problem solve together in order to get the task accomplished.

After each group has had time to find objects, ask the children to return to the area in your classroom designated for group discussions. In this area, set up three bins marked *large*, *medium*, and *small*. Ask the peer groups to sort the objects into the appropriate bins, and then begin the larger group discussion.

---

**Step 2:** Using the compass, choose a conceptual reasoning path (or paths).

**Reasoning path (or paths):**     Math

---

**Step 3: Map Out Open-Ended Questions**

Remember that children's conceptual development is driven by your elaborating and questioning during the feedback loops. The ultimate goal is to get children to think deeply, using the skills associated with each conceptual path. So it is important to continue the conversation beyond peer group and into larger classroom discussions. Write down open-ended questions from each category in the question trail (gathering information, analyzing, and brainstorming). Use these questions to kick-start larger group discussions in which children report to the class on what they have found.

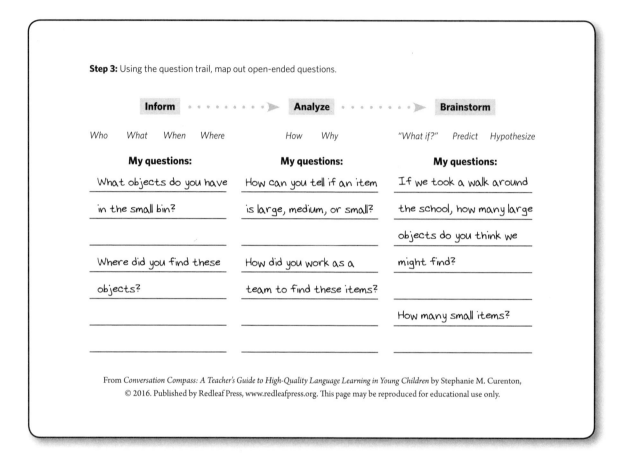

**Step 3:** Using the question trail, map out open-ended questions.

| Inform | Analyze | Brainstorm |
|---|---|---|
| *Who    What    When    Where* | *How    Why* | *"What if?"    Predict    Hypothesize* |
| **My questions:** | **My questions:** | **My questions:** |
| What objects do you have in the small bin? | How can you tell if an item is large, medium, or small? | If we took a walk around the school, how many large objects do you think we might find? |
| Where did you find these objects? | How did you work as a team to find these items? | How many small items? |

From *Conversation Compass: A Teacher's Guide to High-Quality Language Learning in Young Children* by Stephanie M. Curenton, © 2016. Published by Redleaf Press, www.redleafpress.org. This page may be reproduced for educational use only.

Here are some suggestions for follow-up conversations with the large group:

◆ Have the groups talk about what they found.

◆ Start a conversation comparing and contrasting the items in the bins.

◆ Make a graph that shows how many small, medium, or large things the group found.

## Give It a Try on Your Own!

Now is the time for you to apply all you have learned so far by creating a map of your own. Below is an example of a high-quality instructional peer conversation in which a teacher, Miss Kate, creates a plan for her conversation about what children do during free-choice time. Use the example to imagine what Miss Kate's map might look like.

• • •

*It is November in a preschool classroom. Miss Kate sits on the carpet with a white-board at her side, her students surrounding her in a circle. Her learning objective is to get children to remember and describe what they did during free-choice. She opens the conversation by asking one child a question.*

MISS KATE: *Andrea, tell me one thing that you did today that you liked. What were you cooking in there?*

ANDREA: *The turkey.*

MISS KATE: *You cooked a turkey in housekeeping today? I think we need to write down how you cooked that turkey. Because I need to know how to cook a turkey for my Thanksgiving feast. Maybe you guys can help me out. Teach me how to cook a turkey.*

ANDREA: *I cook by myself.*

MISS KATE: *How do you cook it, Andrea?* [She prepares to write on the whiteboard.]

ANDREA: *In the stove.*

MISS KATE: *Put it in the stove. For how long?*

ANDREA: *Two hours.*

MISS KATE: *For two hours.*

LISA: *One hour.*

MISS KATE: *One hour.* [The two children argue over whether it should cook for one hour or two.] *Well, it depends really on how big your turkey is, right? If we had a little turkey, you cook it less amount of time than if it's a really big turkey. The turkey we had in housekeeping today, was it big or little?*

LISA: *Big.*

MISS KATE: *It was big. It might have to cook for five hours. No, it was bigger than that.* [She says to a child who holds up his hands to show the size of the turkey.] *Yeah, it was about that big.* [Teacher demonstrates with hands to show size of turkey.]

• • •

Miss Kate's conversation showed great markers of an instructional conversation. She kept the conversation going through a feedback loop—she cycled through asking open-ended questions, listening, and mirroring. Miss Kate's example was also strong because it was clear she had planned to write down the children's responses about what they had done in free-choice time. She had the whiteboard ready, and she capitalized on Andrea's comment by turning it into an emergent literacy activity by writing the recipe down. She probed the children to think more deeply by asking analyzing questions ("How do you cook it?") and encouraging hypothetical reasoning ("If we had a little turkey ..."). When Lisa chimed into the conversation with a differing opinion about how long to cook the turkey, Miss Kate even modeled how to resolve differing opinions by evaluating the circumstances needed for each to be true ("It really depends on how big your turkey is ...").

## Stop and Consider: Mapping Miss Kate's Conversation

Outline what you imagine Miss Kate's map would look like by answering the following questions.

What do you think her peer group activity was?

_____

_____

_____

_____

_____

Which conceptual reasoning path do you think she chose as a learning objective?

_____

_____

_____

_____

_____

What open-ended questions did she use?

_____

_____

_____

_____

Here is Miss Kate's map:

# The Conversation Map

*Use this form to plan your instructional peer conversation. Follow each step and write down your plan.*

• • • • • • •

**Step 1:** Select and explain the activity and set up the peer groups (2–4 children).

**Activity:** Socio-dramatic play with themes (Thanksgiving theme in house area)

| Group 1 | Group 2 | Group 3 | Group 4 | Group 5 | Group 6 |
|---|---|---|---|---|---|
| Lisa | Richard | Tamara | Ariel | | |
| Andrea | Ray | Shari | Darlene | | |
| Robyn | Izzy | Samir | Shea | | |
| | | | | | |

**Step 2:** Using the compass, choose a conceptual reasoning path (or paths).

**Reasoning path (or paths):** Social

**Step 3:** Using the Question Trail, map out open-ended questions.

| **Inform** • • • • • ➤ | **Analyze** • • • • • ➤ | **Brainstorm** |
|---|---|---|
| *Who   What   When   Where* | *How   Why* | *"What if?"   Predict   Hypothesize* |
| **My questions:** | **My questions:** | **My questions:** |
| For how long do you cook it? | How do you cook it? | If we had a big turkey, how long would we need to cook it? |

Did your answers to the questions match Miss Kate's map? Even if your responses were a little different, take heart! There is no right or wrong way to plan a conversation. You have to plan your conversations based on the needs and personalities of your students and yourself. Two teachers will almost never come up with the same activity, the same conceptual path, and the same questions. Remember, these instructional peer conversations are a journey, and the children are leading the way!

## Wrap It Up

Making the intentional effort to plan instructional peer conversations will build children's knowledge of academic concepts and use of academic language. The Conversation Compass approach makes this easy by offering two tools that can guide your planning. If you use the Compass as a guide and follow the three steps on the map, you can set children, and yourself, on a path toward success.

# Monitoring the Progress of Instructional Peer Conversations

How will you know if your instructional peer conversations are working? The fruits of your hard work and thoughtful planning around conversations may not be seen until weeks or even months later. When it comes to conversations, it is best to keep track of children's changes over time. What can you do to document students' growth in order to keep track of how they are improving?

## How Will You Know If Your Instructional Peer Conversations Are Working?

Progress monitoring is a way to routinely observe and record how children's conversation skills are improving. In progress monitoring, you conduct observations and record information on children's growth and development to try to understand what children have learned (Olson et al. 2007; Fuchs and Fuchs 2004). Conducting progress monitoring on conversations provides you with important information about how children are developing their speaking skills and their ability to communicate with peers. Not only is progress monitoring good for children, it is also good for teachers. Research by Landry and her colleagues (2009) shows that when teachers use progress monitoring, their instruction improves. Gathering progress monitoring information about classroom conversations can teach you three things:

1.  how well children are progressing in their language and communication skills;

2.  what skills children still need to learn or improve upon; and

3.  what changes *you* need to make in your teaching to make your instructional conversations more effective.

Investing the time and energy into progress monitoring has important payoffs. In the end, it can help you improve your teaching practices. You can use progress monitoring to generate ideas about the content you might teach (or reteach) in the future. Or you can use this information to figure out how to modify your instruction to meet the needs of different children.

Let's follow Ms. Lisa as she monitors the progress of her preschoolers' conversation skills. We begin the journey with Ms. Lisa as she starts to wonder if her classroom conversation efforts are working.

● ● ●

*Ms. Lisa has been working hard to apply the Conversation Compass approach, but she is not sure if it is working for her class. It seems like the talkative children are talking a little more during group discussion but she cannot tell if the quiet children are. She has no idea if there have been changes in how the children talk with each other.*

● ● ●

## Stop and Consider: Observing Children's Conversation Skills

Observing children's growth in peer conversation skills is harder than observing growth in traditional academic skills, like literacy or math, because there are no set benchmarks. Listening and watching children during child-led peer conversations is the only way to truly understand how children's conversation skills are growing.

How could Ms. Lisa find out if, and how, children are talking with their peers?

_____

_____

_____

_____

_____

How could she be sure the quiet children were talking with their peers during playtime and small-group activities?

_____

_____

_____

_____

_____

_____

# How Do You Conduct Progress Monitoring?

Conducting progress monitoring for conversations does not have to be difficult if you make it a part of your normal classroom routine. The observations and recordings you make of children's instructional conversations should be simple and easy to track. When you are ready to start monitoring children's progress, there are a few tools and approaches you can use. And the first step in progress monitoring is deciding to make the effort.

• • •

*Ms. Lisa decides that over the next two weeks, she will make special efforts to observe children in her class, watching how they talk with their peers and how they respond during circle time and small-group discussions. She will also make an effort to talk one-on-one with each child throughout the week, both to get first hand knowledge of their conversation skills and to build a personal relationship with her students.*

• • •

## Progress Monitoring:
## Observing Children during Play and Small-Group Work

It is important to observe how children work and play with their peers. You can make such observations every day. During observations, make note of certain important things:

### WHAT TO WATCH WHEN OBSERVING PEER WORK AND PLAY

   **1. Notice if a child approaches other children to engage in a conversation.** Does the child have one special friend that she always approaches? If so, does this special friend speak the same home language as the child? During what type of learning activity does the child typically approach her peers (for instance, free-choice or outside play)?

**2. Notice if the child is engaged in conversations with a variety of CALD learners.** Does the child have conversations with both boys and girls? Does the child engage in conversations with children who are racially and ethnically different from him? Does the child attempt to talk with children whose home language is different from his own?

**3. Notice how long the child is engaged in conversation with peers.** Does the child stay in a conversation with a peer for at least ten minutes, or are most of her conversations with other children brief? Does the child engage in conversations about pretend or fantasy play with other children? During play interactions, are her comments relevant to the topic the other children are talking about? Does the child pick up on the pretend/fantasy components of a conversation and build on them?

As you are observing children during their work and play, you may notice that some children are quieter than others. This is your opportunity to modify your teaching practices by finding intentional strategies to bring these quieter children into the conversation.

**Bridge from Home to School:**
**Encouraging Quiet CALD Learners to Talk during Conversations**

All children have unique language abilities and personalities. Many culturally and linguistically diverse (CALD) children have another unique experience they bring to the classroom: their home language experiences. Some CALD children may be from homes where everyone speaks Arabic. Other children may have parents who speak English, but have a live-in grandmother who speaks only Hindi. Still another child may live with a mother who speaks French and a father who speaks Haitian Creole. All children's uniquenesses—personalities, language abilities, and home languages—result in diverse conversation styles (see chapter 1). You should expect that children will behave differently during conversations. Here are some suggestions for how you might modify your conversation practices to fit the needs of CALD children who are quiet during conversations.

- Learn to use a few key words from the child's home language, especially words that refer to children's basic needs (*potty, eat, sleep/nap*) or words/expressions that help you and the child establish a social bond (*Good job!, hug, please, thank you*).

- Teach the child's peers these key words and encourage them to use the words around the classroom.
- When the child is new to the classroom, if possible, pair the child with others who speak the same home language in order to avoid the child becoming linguistically isolated.
- At first, when the child is new to the classroom, encourage the child to engage in games and activities with peers that don't require a lot of speaking.
- Group the child with talkative peers who have learned a few key words in the CALD child's home language.
- Later, as their English language skills become stronger, encourage the child to become involved in pretend play with peers.
- Give the child leadership roles and responsibilities that do not require lots of talking.
- After their language skills have become stronger, encourage the child to share personal stories with peers.
- Do not judge children when they engage in code-switching between two languages/dialects.

## Progress Monitoring: Track Peer Conversations

One of the easiest ways to record your observations is with a simple Tracking Peer Conversations form. You can use this tool to take notes while observing children interacting with peers in socio-dramatic play scenarios or during small-group work activities. Be sure that the setting for the conversation you are observing is a child-led activity in which two to four children are free to choose their play partners and are responsible for maintaining their own interactions. It's best to find a time and space that allows you to observe without interfering with the interactions.

For example, if you are observing a small group of children playing in the house area, you can grab a few copies of the Tracking Peer Conversation form and find a good observation distance. Take on the role of silent observer and make notes for every child involved. In this case, position yourself on the outside of the group, far enough away so that children won't feel compelled to involve you but close enough to hear well.

# Tracking Peer Conversations

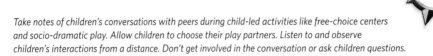

*Take notes of children's conversations with peers during child-led activities like free-choice centers and socio-dramatic play. Allow children to choose their play partners. Listen to and observe children's interactions from a distance. Don't get involved in the conversation or ask children questions.*

• • • • • • •

**Date of Observation:** February 23, 2016        **Name of Observer:** Ms. Lisa

| Names of Playmates | Play activity | Describe the children's conversation strengths and challenges. |
|---|---|---|
| Antonio<br>José<br>Akeem | House area/pretend play<br>(Blocks)<br>Playground<br>Computers<br>Art | Engaged in a lively debate about how to construct a bridge. Antonio took the lead by suggesting what job the other boys should do. José did not talk as much as others but was fully engaged and busy stacking blocks. Akeem asked lots of questions and had great sound effects. Boys had fun together. |
| Anna<br>Gita<br>Sonali | (House area/pretend play)<br>Blocks<br>Playground<br>Computers<br>Art | Girls had an argument over who could be the princess. Gita stutters a little and the girls have a hard time understanding. She got mad and started to shout. Sonali reminded Gita to use her inside voice. Anna suggested they each be a princess and gave Gita a doll and that made Gita happy. |

In the Tracking Peer Conversations example, Ms. Lisa noted several things she thought were important. For example, in the conversation between Antonio, José, and Akeem, she noted (a) how much each child talked, (b) whether a child asked questions, (c) the boys' emotions while playing, (d) whether or not José's playmates seemed to understand him, (e) whether or not a child was the cause of any unresolved conflicts, and (f) if each boy was actively engaged and cooperative during the interaction. Making notes such as this will help you understand children's communication skills and provide you with insight into how to help a child develop his skills.

## Progress Monitoring: Dictate a Discussion

Another progress monitoring activity you can use to gauge children's conversation skills is dictating a discussion. Use a whiteboard or flip chart to take notes about the key points that children bring up during discussions. For example, if they are engaged in a discussion about words that begin with the letter *p*, then you can write down all the words they generate. If you use this technique repeatedly throughout the year with multiple letters, then these notes will serve not only as evidence of how much children talked but also of how their vocabulary has grown.

Use dictation to engage children in a discussion about a story and record their responses. You can ask them about key elements of a story: the plot (what's this story about), setting (where does this story take place), characters (who is in the story), and the character's motive (what is the character trying to do).

## Progress Monitoring: Record a Conversation

A third way to monitor children's progress is by recording conversations. Before you start a conversation, tell the children that you are going to be recording what they say so you can listen to it later. You can audio-record them participating in peer conversations. Then you can listen to the recording and make note of their conversation skills based on what you hear. You can even use this audio recording to complete a Tracking Peer Conversations sheet later.

You can play back the audio recording to the students and have them listen to their own conversation. Replaying the recording serves as a listening activity that teaches children to fine-tune their receptive skills. Try recording a conversation and replaying it for children a few days later. Ask them questions about who said what and what else they remember about that conversation. The discussion of the recording becomes a *meta-conversation*: a present conversation about a past conversation. Engaging in meta-conversations can help develop children's mental representation skills, understanding of language, and memory.

## Bridge from Home to School: Proceed with Caution When Monitoring the Progress of CALD Learners

When you are monitoring the progress of culturally linguistically diverse (CALD) learners, you should remember several things. First, consider how they are engaging in conversations and match their skills with the instructional and peer support they may need. For example, children who speak only their home language may need to be routinely paired with other CALD children who speak the same language. This will help to ensure that they are not isolated during peer conversations. On the other hand, if children are beginning to use some words in English and attempting to answer questions at circle time, then they can be paired with socially talkative, English-speaking peers, who can serve as peer language models.

Second, remember that those CALD children who speak a different home language may be quiet at first, but eventually they may become more talkative as they become stronger communicators in English. Give those children time to warm up to the classroom. Delay conducting progress monitoring until they have been in the classroom for a few weeks and have developed a solid friendship with at least one peer.

Third, focus on helping CALD children develop the vocabulary words to express their ideas rather than on the grammatical structures they use—in other words, focus on *what* they're able to say rather than *how* they say it. During the preschool period, all children are developing their understanding of the grammatical structure of English, so they all will make grammatical mistakes when speaking. Respond to CALD students by simply mirroring back their words using correct grammar. A child might say, "He breaked the crayon," and all you need to say is, "He broke the crayon?" and then continue on with the conversation: "How did he do that?"

## Wrap It Up

Progress monitoring is an ongoing cycle of recorded observation that you should practice frequently with all your students. This progress monitoring is helpful to you as a teacher because it provides you with a record of children's growth. You can use the monitoring information to think about ways to improve your practice and keep the conversation going!

Thank you for taking this journey to learn about the Conversation Compass approach. If you use what you learned along with the planning tools, your classroom will be filled with chatty children who love talking with each other and working in peer groups. I hope that this approach has shown you that teachers are the navigators but children are the drivers of conversation. With a little practice, you can incorporate the Conversation Compass approach in the life of your classroom every day.

Go forth and converse!

# APPENDIX:
# REPRODUCIBLE TOOLS

How Is Your Child Talking at Home?

The Feedback Loop

The Question Trail

The Compass

The Conversation Map

Tracking Peer Conversations

# How Is Your Child Talking at Home?

Dear _____ ,

During school, your child will spend a lot of time talking with classmates. I encourage the students to talk about their ideas, opinions, and feelings. I want them to feel free to express themselves. Can you help me learn more about how your child talks at home?

Child's Name: _____    Date of Birth: _____

## Language(s) Spoken at Home

What language(s) or dialect(s) are spoken in your home? _____

_____

Who speaks to your child in this language(s)/dialect(s)? _____

_____

Do you or a family member ever make up stories and tell them to your child?    ❏ Yes   ❏ No

Do you or a family member ever tell your child stories about things you did when you were his or her age?
❏ Yes   ❏ No

Does your child ever make up stories and tell them to you?    ❏ Yes   ❏ No

Does your child like to be read to?    ❏ Yes   ❏ No

Does your child pretend to read or try to read when given reading materials?    ❏ Yes   ❏ No

How many children's books do you have in your house?

*fewer than 10*          *10-20*          *20-40*          *more than 40*

In what language(s) are the children's books?_____

_____

How many times in the past week have you read a storybook to your child?

*Not at all*          *once*          *2-3 times*          *4 or more*

About how old was your child the first time you read to him/her?

*less than 1 yr old*          *1-2 yrs old*          *3-4 yrs old*

# How Is Your Child Talking at Home? (continued)

Do you like to read?　❏ *Yes*　❏ *No*

In which language(s) do you like to read? _____

_____

What's the name of your child's favorite book? _____

_____

Is your child allowed to use the computer, tablet, e-reader, or smartphone?　❏ *Yes*　❏ *No*

How many hours per day does your child spend playing on the computer, tablet, e-reader, or smartphone?

_____

How many hours per day does your child spend watching TV? _____

What is your child's favorite TV program? _____

_____

# The Feedback Loop

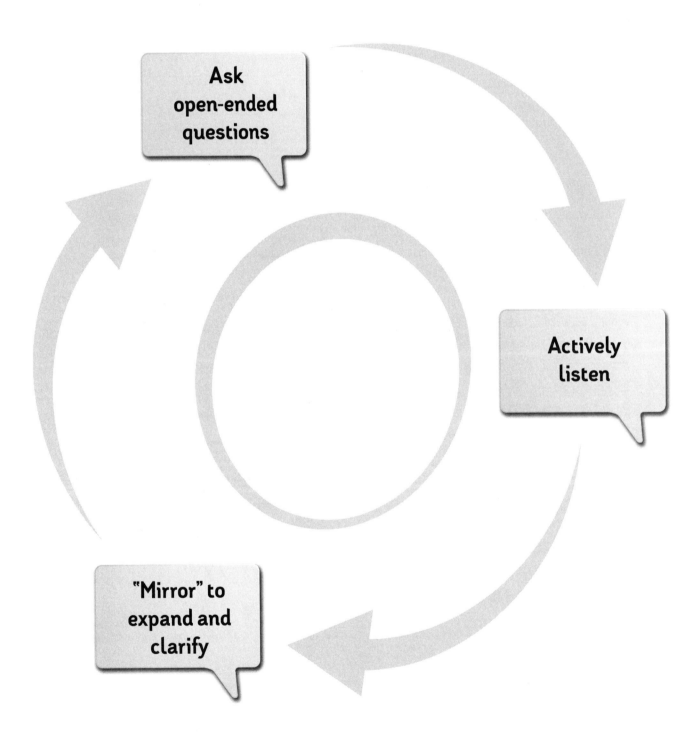

Ask open-ended questions

Actively listen

"Mirror" to expand and clarify

# The Question Trail

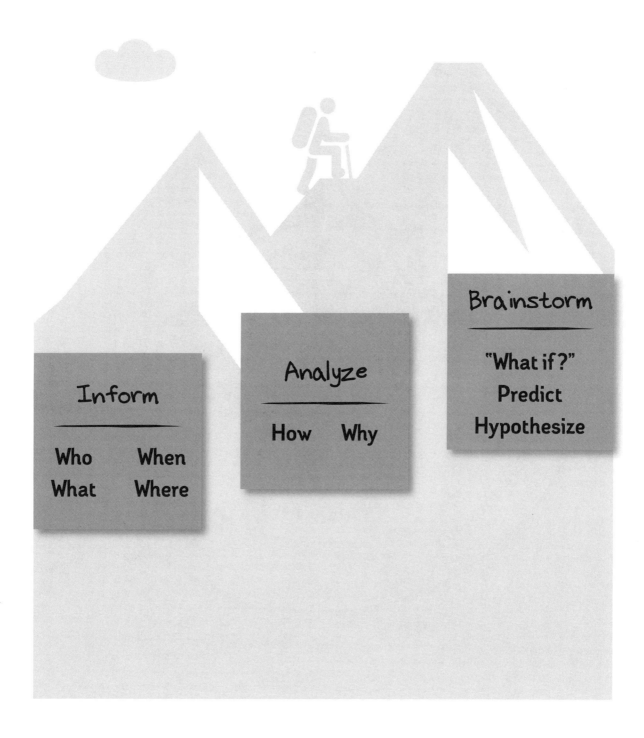

**Inform**

Who    When
What    Where

**Analyze**

How    Why

**Brainstorm**

"What if?"
Predict
Hypothesize

# Conversation Compass

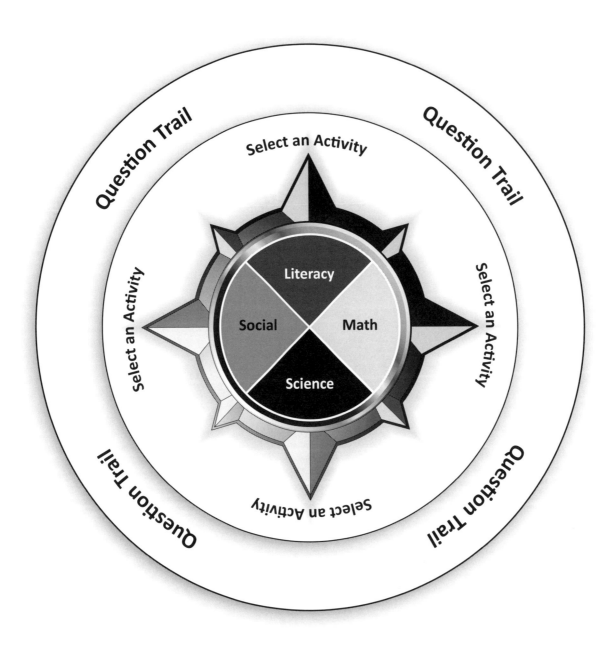

# The Conversation Map

*Use this form to plan your instructional peer conversation. Follow each step and write down your plan.*

• • • • • • • •

**Step 1:** Select and explain the activity and set up the peer groups (2–4 children).

**Activity:**

| Group 1 | Group 2 | Group 3 | Group 4 | Group 5 | Group 6 |
|---------|---------|---------|---------|---------|---------|
| _____ | _____ | _____ | _____ | _____ | _____ |
| _____ | _____ | _____ | _____ | _____ | _____ |
| _____ | _____ | _____ | _____ | _____ | _____ |
| _____ | _____ | _____ | _____ | _____ | _____ |

**Step 2:** Using the compass, choose a conceptual reasoning path (or paths).

**Reasoning path (or paths):**

**Step 3:** Using the Question Trail, map out open-ended questions.

| **Inform** · · · · · · · ▶ | **Analyze** · · · · · · · ▶ | **Brainstorm** |
|---|---|---|
| *Who    What    When    Where* | *How    Why* | *"What if?"    Predict    Hypothesize* |
| **My questions:** | **My questions:** | **My questions:** |

# Tracking Peer Conversations

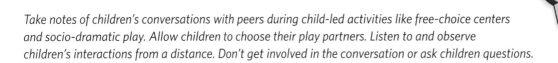

*Take notes of children's conversations with peers during child-led activities like free-choice centers and socio-dramatic play. Allow children to choose their play partners. Listen to and observe children's interactions from a distance. Don't get involved in the conversation or ask children questions.*

• • • • • • •

**Date of Observation:** _____     **Name of Observer:** _____

| Names of Playmates | Play activity | Describe the children's conversation strengths and challenges. |
|---|---|---|
| _____ <br> _____ <br> _____ <br> _____ | House area/pretend play <br><br> Blocks <br><br> Playground <br><br> Computers <br><br> Art | |
| _____ <br> _____ <br> _____ <br> _____ | House area/pretend play <br><br> Blocks <br><br> Playground <br><br> Computers <br><br> Art | |

# REFERENCES

Beneke, Margaret, and Gregory A. Cheatham. 2015. "Speaking up for African American English: Equity and Inclusion in Early Childhood Settings." *Early Childhood Education Journal* 43 (1): 127–134.

Cabell, Sonia Q., Laura M. Justice, Shayne B. Piasta, Stephanie M. Curenton, Alice Wiggins, Khara Pence Turnbull, and Yaacov Petscher. 2011. "The Impact of Teacher Responsivity Education on Preschoolers' Language and Literacy Skills." *American Journal of Speech-Language Pathology* 20 (4): 315–330.

Chapman, Robin S. 2000. "Children's Language Learning: An Interactionist Perspective." *Journal of Child Psychology and Psychiatry* 41 (1): 33–54.

Collier, Mary Jane. 1988. "A Comparison of Conversations among and between Domestic Culture Groups: How Intra- and Intercultural Competencies Vary." *Communication Quarterly* 36 (2): 122–144.

Common Core State Standards Initiative. 2015. "Common Core Standards for English Language Arts and Literacy." http://www.corestandards.org/ELA-Literacy/SL/K/.

Connor, Carol McDonald, Frederick J. Morrison, and Lisa Slominski. 2006. "Preschool Instruction and Children's Emergent Literacy Growth." *Journal of Educational Psychology* 98 (4): 665–689.

Crystal, David. 2010. *Cambridge Encyclopedia of Language*. 3rd ed. Cambridge: Cambridge University Press.

Dickinson, David K. 2001. "Large-Group and Free-Play Times: Conversational Settings Supporting Language and Literacy Development." In *Beginning Literacy with Language: Young Children Learning at Home and School*, edited by David Dickinson and Patton Tabors, 223–255. Baltimore, MD: Brookes.

Early, Diane Marie, Iheoma U. Iruka, Sharon Ritchie, Oscar A. Barbarin, Donna-Marie C. Winn, Gisele M. Crawford, Pamela M. Frome, Richard M. Clifford, Margaret Burchinal, Carollee Howes, Donna M. Bryant, and Robert C. Pianta. 2010. "How Do Pre-Kindergarteners Spend Their Time? Gender,

Ethnicity, and Income as Predictors of Experiences in Pre-Kindergarten Classrooms." *Early Childhood Research Quarterly* 25 (2): 177–193. doi:10.1016/j.ecresq.2009.10.003

Fivush, Robyn, and Qi Wang. 2005. "Emotion Talk in Mother-Child Conversations of the Shared Past: The Effects of Culture, Gender, and Event Valence." *Journal of Cognition and Development* 6 (4): 489–506.

Fuchs, Lynn S., and Douglas Fuchs. 2004. "Determining Adequate Yearly Progress from Kindergarten through Grade 6 with Curriculum-Based Measurement." *Assessment for Effective Intervention* 29 (4): 25–37.

Garrod, Simon, and Martin J. Pickering. 2004. "Why Is Conversation so Easy?" *TRENDS in Cognitive Sciences* 8 (1): 8–11.

Gest, Scott D., Rebecca Holland-Coviello, Janet A. Welsh, Deborah L. Eicher-Catt, and Sukhdeep Gill. 2006. "Language Development Subcontexts in Head Start Classrooms: Distinctive Patterns of Teacher Talk During Free Play, Mealtime, and Book Reading." *Early Education and Development* 17 (2): 293–315.

Halliday, M. A. K. 2004. *The Language of Early Childhood*, vol. 4. New York: Bloomsbury Academic.

Henry, Gary. T., and Dana K. Rickman. 2007. "Do Peers Influence Children's Skill Development in Preschool?" *Economics of Education Review* 26 (1): 100–112.

Justice, Laura M., Andrew Mashburn, Khara L. Pence, and Alice Wiggins. 2008. "Experimental Evaluation of a Preschool Language Curriculum: Influence on Children's Expressive Language Skills." *Journal of Speech, Language, and Hearing Research* 51 (4): 983–1001.

Justice, Laura M., Yaacov Petscher, Christopher Schatschneider, and Andrew Mashburn. 2011. "Peer Effects in Preschool Classrooms: Is Children's Language Growth Associated With Their Classmates' Skills?" *Child Development* 82 (6): 1768–1777.

Landry, Susan H., Jason L. Anthony, Paul R. Swank, and Pauline Monseque-Bailey. 2009. "Effectiveness of Comprehensive Professional Development for Teachers of At-Risk Preschoolers." *Journal of Educational Psychology* 101 (2): 448–465.

McCabe, Allyssa, and Lynn S. Bliss. 2002. *Patterns of Narrative Discourse: A Multicultural, Life Span Approach*. Boston: Pearson.

Moll, Luis C., and Norma González. 1994. "Lessons from Research with Language-Minority Children." *Journal of Reading Behavior* 26 (4): 439–456.

National Research Council. 2000. *Eager to Learn: Educating Our Preschoolers,* edited by Barbara T. Bowman, M. Suzanne Donovan, and M. Susan Burns. Washington, DC: National Academy Press.

Olson, Stephanie C., Edward J. Daly III, Melissa Andersen, April Turner, and Courtney LeClair. 2007. "Assessing Student Response to Intervention." In *Handbook of Response to Intervention: The Science and Practice of Assessment and Intervention,* edited by Shane R. Jimerson, Matthew K. Burns, and Amanda M. VanDerHeyden, 117–129. New York: Springer.

Pence, Khara L., Laura M. Justice, and Alice K. Wiggins. 2008. "Preschool Teachers' Fidelity in Implementing a Comprehensive Language-Rich Curriculum." *Language, Speech, and Hearing Services in Schools* 39 (3): 329–341.

Pianta, Robert C., Karen M. LaParo, and Bridget K. Hamre. 2008. *Classroom Assessment Scoring System for Pre-K.* Baltimore, MD: Brookes.

Piasta, Shayne B., Laura M. Justice, Sonia Q. Cabell, Alice K. Wiggins, Khara Pence Turnbull, and Stephanie M. Curenton. 2012. "Impact of Professional Development on Preschool Teachers' Conversational Responsivity and Children's Linguistic Productivity and Complexity." *Early Childhood Research Quarterly* 27 (3): 387–400.

Rogoff, Barbara. 1994. "Developing Understanding of the Idea of Communities of Learners." *Mind, Culture, and Activity* 1 (4): 209–229.

Schechter, Carlota, and Beth Bye. 2007. "Preliminary Evidence for the Impact of Mixed-Income Preschools on Low-Income Children's Language Growth." *Early Childhood Research Quarterly* 22 (1): 137–146.

van Kleeck, Anne. 2014. "Distinguishing Between Casual Talk and Academic Talk Beginning in the Preschool Years: An Important Consideration for Speech-Language Pathologists." *American Journal of Speech-Language Pathology* 23 (4): 724–741.

Vygotsky, Lev S. (1934) 1987. "Thinking and Speech." In *The Collected Works of L. S. Vygotsky,* 39–285. Vol. 1, *Problems of General Psychology.* New York: Plenum Press. Edited by Robert W. Rieber and Aaron S. Carton. Translated by Norris Minick.

Weitzman, Elaine, and Janice Greenberg. 2002. *Learning Language and Loving It: A Guide to Promoting Children's Social, Language and Literacy Development.* Toronto: Hanen Centre.

Zepeda, Marlene, Dina C. Castro, and Sharon Cronin. 2011. "Preparing Early Childhood Teachers to Work with Young Dual Language Learners." *Child Development Perspectives* 5 (1): 10–14.